Piaget and Education
PRIMER

PETER LANG
New York • Washington, D.C./Baltimore • Bern
Frankfurt am Main • Berlin • Brussels • Vienna • Oxford

David W. Jardine

Piaget & Education
PRIMER

PETER LANG
New York • Washington, D.C./Baltimore • Bern
Frankfurt am Main • Berlin • Brussels • Vienna • Oxford

KH

Library of Congress Cataloging-in-Publication Data

Jardine, David William.
Piaget and education primer/ David W. Jardine
p. cm.
Includes bibliographical references.
1. Cognitive learning. 2. Piaget, Jean, 1896- . 3. Cognition in children.
4. Genetic epistemology. I. Title.
LB1590.3.J37 2006   370.15'23—dc22   2005032910
ISBN 0-8204-7261-1

Bibliographic information published by **Die Deutsche Bibliothek**.
Die Deutsche Bibliothek lists this publication in the "Deutsche
Nationalbibliografie"; detailed bibliographic data is available
on the Internet at http://dnb.ddb.de/.

The paper in this book meets the guidelines for permanence and durability
of the Committee on Production Guidelines for Book Longevity
of the Council of Library Resources.

© 2006 Peter Lang Publishing, Inc., New York
29 Broadway, New York, NY 10006
www.peterlangusa.com

Printed in the United States of America

10/18/17

Table of Contents

CHAPTER ONE

Introduction

Imagine a bright summer's day, brilliant sun and blue skies. An eighteen-month-old child is watching her mother blow soap bubbles. As the bubbles float up into the air, the child smiles and claps her hands, breaking some bubbles, giggling and chasing down others that have eluded her.

Now imagine that this clapping, giggling and chasing are not simply wonderful instances of the ebullience of the young. According to Jean Piaget, these are also acts of knowledge: the very sort of actions essential to the eventual mastering of mathematics and logic, foundational for the sciences generally in terms of their methodologies, even, he claims, foundational to the emergence of intelligence itself. Such clapping, giggling and chasing may not yet be fully formed acts of comprehension, but they are, according to Piaget, clearly acts of *prehension,* through which knowledge is experienced in a way familiar to us all: as grasping something, getting a hold of something, coming to grips with something.

This simple vignette reveals how the work of Jean Piaget has influenced educational theory and practice. His work has had a widespread influence on how we observe and interpret the lives of children, even those of us who have come across his work only in charts of "stages of development" in some child-psychology textbook. Many textbooks include a common image of Piaget: a white-haired old man with his pipe, wearing glasses, a beret and a kindly expression.

The Commonsense Legacy of Jean Piaget's Work

An astonishing number of near commonsensical beliefs in educational theory and practice owe their origins directly or indirectly to Jean Piaget's legacy, including the beliefs that:

- children go through stages of development, and one must be sensitive to "where the child is at";
- a student should be presented with materials and curricular expectations appropriate to the stage of development he or she is at;
- the development of intelligence occurs not only in stages, but in a traceable *sequence* of stages;
- developmentally appropriate curriculum materials must therefore also be sequenced to fit the stages of the development of intelligence in the child;
- in any real classroom, individual children will be at different levels of development;
- "ages" and "stages" and "grade levels" are not equivalent except as very broad generalizations that are, more often than not, overgeneralizations;
- in order to learn, young children especially (but not exclusively) are greatly helped by active manipulation of objects (an early thread of hands-on learning);
- children sometimes need to use concrete materials (objects, images, examples, visual or auditory aids, etc.) not only to learn, but also to show, demonstrate or articulate what they have learned;

- experiencing and knowing the world in deeply embodied, sensory, playful and image-filled ways are ways of being intelligent (a thread of what has come to be known as "multiple intelligences" (Gardner 2000)
- children's play is a central feature of the development of intelligence;
- the healthy establishment of a previous stage is necessary to the healthy achievement of the next stage; and finally,
- in knowing the world, we don't just take in the world passively—rather, we actively construct our experiences and understandings of the world according to our own concepts, categories, levels of development and previous experiences.

Whether or not we explicitly and intentionally identify with Jean Piaget's beliefs, as students, teachers, parents, administrators, curriculum planners and educational theorists and researchers, we are already living out his legacy in the day-to-day practice of education in North America.

The purpose of this book is to explore the nature and origins of Piaget's ideas. As we shall see, even seemingly simple, straightforward educational practices—like the pedagogical allowance given to that eighteen-month-old girl and her bubble pursuits—can have long, mysterious, sometimes ancient roots. As we unearth those roots in the following chapters, I hope those involved in education will get a glimpse of Jean Piaget's generous contribution to our ability to be thoughtful about children and careful in our claims about what they know and how they come to know it.

In Lieu of a Biography

There are plenty of biographical sketches available on the life of Jean Piaget, so for our purposes here, the briefest sketch will suffice. Piaget was born on August 9, 1896 in Neuchâtel, Switzerland, and died on September 16, 1980. Young Jean was extremely precocious, publishing his first paper in 1907, at

the age of eleven. A very brief observational note regarding a particular sparrow indigenous to his native Switzerland, it was entitled "An Albino Sparrow." Over the course of his life, Piaget wrote over sixty books and hundreds of articles, ranging from studies in biology and zoology to works on child development, logic, mathematics and philosophy. By 1955, he became the founder and director of the International Centre for Genetic Epistemology in Geneva, where the work he originated is carried on to this day.

Two biographical events are of special importance in understanding the nature and ancestry of Piaget's lifework and the sort of breakthrough his work made.

First, Piaget started work in standardized intelligence testing. Shortly after receiving his doctorate in 1918 (at age twenty-two), he began "working for Théodore Simon, co-author of the Binet-Simon intelligence scale. Simon placed him in Binet's laboratory, and set him to work standardizing Cyril Burt's reasoning tests on Parisian children" (Indiana University 2005). This biographical tidbit is by itself enough to catch the attention of educators, inundated as is our profession is with standardized intelligence tests of all shapes and sizes. But what happened next was transforming: Piaget "began to notice that children of similar ages made similar types of mistakes, and it occurred to him that Simon, Binet and Burt might be asking the wrong question: Perhaps the key to understanding human intellectual development is not in *what* children get wrong, but *how* they get it wrong" (Indiana University 2005).

As educators, we know how easy it is to ask the wrong questions in our work with students. We've all felt the frustration, as well, of having to administer tests that did not allow our students to show what they know. Jean Piaget noticed, in his attempts to standardize the results of the intelligence tests, that the tests could not account for what was really going on. It was not simply that the types of mistakes made by four-year-old or eight-year-old children

were interesting. What was more significant was that by age twelve, most children had stopped making those types of mistakes altogether. Therefore, instead of "taking the ready-made **schema** of adult reasoning (and of explicit scientific or legal reasoning at that) and submitting this schema, to, say, syllogistic tests to see whether the child conforms to our practical or scholastic habits of thought" (Piaget, 1972a, p. 135)—which only allows us to map children's failures to achieve those standards—perhaps we should be looking at how children actually think. It may make good sense, therefore, to not call intelligence-test results "mistakes" at all. Children's answers may somehow be "correct," that is, proper to a type of thinking that the tests do not measure.

Even more profound was Piaget's suggestion that children's thinking, reasoning and experience are not just failures to achieve adult standards and expectations but are substantially different from adult thinking and experience in their character. Children's thinking, reasoning and experience may have integrity and truth that is masked if we leave typical adult thinking in place as the unforgiving norm against which children are understood, judged and taught. We can add this to the Piagetian legacy: an early disruption of what has been called "adultomorphism" (Ausubel, Sullivan & Ives, 1980, p. 374): a longstanding tendency to map children's lives against the shape or morphology of adulthood and see nothing but deficiencies and lack. It is not enough, Piaget's work suggests, to consider children (or adults, in fact) as empty vessels to be filled, passively and repetitively, with what they lack. Children, like adults, are active agents in coming to know the world, agents that *make* something of their experiences.

A second biographical event dovetails with Piaget's work in testing in fascinating ways. In 1925, right in the midst of his burgeoning insight that children may think differently, Jean Piaget's first child, Jacqueline, was born. She (and her siblings to follow) became the subject of intense systematic observations

Schema/schemata

Piaget's term for a structure, category or organization of thought or action.

in her early years, and Jean Piaget became an astute, meticulous observer of children and their behaviour, actions and interactions. As a result of his insights, early childhood educators today look with greater intensity at, for example, a young child manipulating some wooden blocks: attempting to get a bridge levelled, eyeing things up, sizing up blocks, trying one out, failing, looking again, knocking it over in frustration, then coming back again and again. All of these, according to Piaget, are great acts of coming to know the world, though they may all too easily be seen as simply "playing around."

In familial interactions with Jacqueline and her siblings, Piaget became skilled as well—perhaps also via his early background in psychology and psychoanalysis (1919–20)—at talking with children, listening carefully to their answers and questions, and then following their leads. Many of his earlier works are based on conversations with children, and they are full of fascinating back-and-forth questioning and answering, exploring and describing.

Recapitulation, Progress and the Search for Origins

Jean Piaget's work emerged out of a vibrant and contested time. The end of the nineteenth and beginning of the twentieth centuries were a burgeoning time for what were called in Europe "the human sciences" and in Germany, *Geisteswissenschaften*—roughly translated, "sciences of the spirit." Anthropology, psychology, sociology, linguistics, to name but a few, were blossoming and were attempting to find their footing as sciences, given the successes of the natural sciences in controlling, predicting and manipulating the physical world. In the midst of this onrush stands education itself, which was beginning to reimagine itself not simply as a set of traditional practices passed on in practice, but as both the object and practice of science, a topic of learned intellectual study. How children learn, what teaching practices are effective, what we should be teaching, how schools should look—all these became

topics investigated by various scientific means, producing, for example, "educational psychology" (education as the object of the science of psychology) and "educational foundations" (education as the object of philosophy).

Jean Piaget was born into this emerging age of the human sciences, an intellectual cradle full of hopes and visions of human life, its nature and its destinies. A full account of this complex era is nearly impossible, but three ideas were in the air then that bear some examination now: progress, recapitulation and origins (see Jardine, 2002). These three ideas came to form the core of Jean Piaget's work, as we shall see shortly, and thus have been inherited by any teacher or student living out the Piagetian legacy.

First, we turn to the work of Ernst Haeckel (1834–1919), a then-renowned biologist, philosopher and social theorist. Central to Haeckel's major work, *The Riddle of the Universe at the Close of the Nineteenth Century* (1900) is the idea of **recapitulation**. He suggested that an exploration of the history and growth of the individual human being, what is called **ontogeny** (from *ontos*, the genesis of the individual being):

Recapitulation

The belief that the stages of development of the individual mirror those of the species, and that studying an individual's development will aid our understanding of the species' development: ontogeny recapitulates phylogeny.

Ontogeny

The genesis, growth or development of the individual.

Phylogeny

The genesis, growth or development of the species.

> [M]ust be completed by a second, equally valuable, and closely connected branch of thought—the history of race (**phylogeny**). Both of these branches of evolutionary science, are, in my opinion, in the closest causal connection; this arises from the reciprocal action of the laws of heredity and adaptation. *Ontogenesis is a brief and rapid recapitulation of phylogenesis,* determined by the physiological functions of heredity (generation) and adaptation (maintenance). (Haeckel, 1900, p. 233, emphasis added)

This spellbinding idea—that the growth and development of the individual recapitulate the growth and development of the species as a whole—fit in well with late-nineteenth-century ideas of progress. At the time, a widespread belief prevailed that European society—especially its achievements in science, industry and technology—represented the crowning jewel of humanity. As we shall discuss in

chapter 5, this belief fit all too well with the Eurocentric ideas of colonialism and empire that fashioned Europe's often brutal relations with the "underdeveloped" world. These ideas, despite their decreased predominance in the twentieth century, left us with the dichotomy of developed versus developing worlds, a conceptualization cast in the belief that our own culture provides the unquestionable model of development for the world.

This image still persists of the child as a being that, in its course of development, recapitulates the progressive development of the species. A wonderful example follows of how the intellectual and imaginal legacies that underwrite Piagetian theory became part of the popular imagination and popular child-rearing practices today:

> Each child as he develops is retracing the whole history of mankind, physically and spiritually, step by step. A baby starts off in the womb as a single tiny cell, just the way the first living thing appeared in the ocean. Weeks later, as he lies in the amniotic fluid of the womb, he has gills like a fish. (Spock & Parker, 1957, p. 223)

What may have seemed like an odd, antiquated, overly philosophical idea is here being re-cited by Benjamin Spock, in what became one of the best-selling books of all time, *Dr. Spock's Baby and Child Care.*

Another equally powerful idea is coupled with recapitulation and development-as-progress in Jean Piaget's intellectual ancestry: the search for origins. Before Haeckel's insight into recapitulation, G.W.F. Hegel had argued that the course of human history has been a history of the struggle of Absolute Spirit becoming, in a series of definable stages, more and more self-aware. Charles Darwin had already suggested, in *On the Origin of Species* (published in 1859), that not only the human species, but all current species on earth have evolved or developed over time. To properly understand ourselves and the other species on earth, therefore, it became necessary to search out how we have become who we are. In the same year, Karl Marx suggested that current

forms of capitalism and other socioeconomic arrangements had emerged over a history of material relations, the exploration of which was essential to our self-understanding. Sigmund Freud (born in 1859, the year *Origin of Species* and *Das Kapital* appeared) introduced a strikingly similar suggestion in his emerging pyschoanalysis, that the health of the adult is rooted in the healthy development of the child into adulthood, and that psychological troubles are consequently rooted in childhood. Thus, Freud suggested, returning patients to the "origin" of their difficulties would pave the way to health and wellbeing.

All of these examples (and many more) became a great series of humiliations. This was an audacious and difficult idea: that we have *become* who we are, both individually (ontogeny) and as a race or society (phylogeny), and that this "becoming" happened in ways far less noble or elevated than our self-satisfied ideas of civility and progress led us to believe. Simply examining who we are and what we believe and do in the present day was no longer an adequate account of ourselves and our world. The sciences, both natural and human, became enamoured of the idea of genesis—*how* we became who we now are, the stepwise emergence of our current beliefs and actions over the long history of humanity. In the human sciences, this led to a widespread search for the *origins* of things:

> [At the end of the nineteenth century] all Western historiography was obsessed with the quest of *origins*. "Origin and development" of something became almost a cliche. Great scholars wrote about the origin of language, of human societies, of art, of institutions, of the Indo-Aryan races, and so on. Suffice it to say that this search for the origins of human institutions and cultural creations prolongs and completes the naturalist's quest for the origin of the species, the biologist's dream of grasping the origin of life, the geologist's and astronomer's endeavour to understand the origin of the Earth and the Universe. One can decipher here the same nostalgia for the "primordial" and the "original." (Eliade, 1968, p. 44, emphasis original)

Mircea Eliade, cited above, was also caught up in this fervour. His work—a detailed phenomenological examination of the mythological and "primitive" origins of religion, including ideas of initiation, sacred spaces, rites and rituals, heroes and villains—became a precursor to the recently popular work of Joseph Campbell. This popularity is itself tied up with late-twentieth-century interest in native cultures and storytelling and other things seemingly more archaic, ancient and "original"/originary—things more lasting than the acquisitions of the pandemic consumerism of the 1970s, 1980s and 1990s. Even the quaint-sounding "back to the land" movement of the 1960s fits here, with all its dreams of getting ourselves "back to the Garden," as a popular song put it. The search for the origins of things was thus always somewhat Edenic and somewhat restorative. It was a search for the perennial, the foundational, the first things, and great romances arose around such searches.

Eliade gives us an insight into how even this late-nineteenth-century, seemingly modern, scientific and rational search for origins and the late-twentieth-century, seemingly Romantic, mythopoetic and heartfelt version of the same sort of search, were themselves mirrored in age-old quests: "[An] exceptional value [is] attributed to a *knowledge of origins*. For the man of archaic societies, that is, knowledge of the origin of each thing . . . confers a kind of magical mastery over it; he knows where to find it and how to make it reappear in the future" (Eliade, 1968, p. 76, emphasis original). Eliade goes on to describe in detail how all religious traditions share this value: all have stories of how things began, where they came from, what were the first things, who the ancestors are and what they can tell us of ourselves and our troubles—tales of our genesis, our becoming. These first things seem more stable, more real, more foundational, more reliable, more "original," and seeking them out seems to give an anchor and a comfort to modern woes. The search for origins is a quest for restoration and renewal.

Here, too, we find hints as to some of the sense of urgency and hope in education's frequent clarion call, "Back to the basics!" But that is another story (see Jardine, Friesen & Clifford, 2003).

These late-nineteenth-century (and still lingering) images of recapitulation, progressive development and the search for origins were profoundly interrupted by three early-twentieth-century events that dashed many of Europe's grandiose hopes for human progress: a failure of modern industry (the sinking of the *Titanic* in 1912); a failure of reason and humanity (World War I, 1914–18, in which achievements of the natural sciences were put to horrifying use); and a failure of modern medicine (the great Spanish influenza pandemic of 1918–20, during which between fifty and one hundred million people died worldwide, five to ten times the death toll of World War I).

In some quarters, these humiliations led to existential meditations (in music, in art, in philosophy, in drama and the literary arts) on human frailty, meditations that continue today. In other quarters, these failures led to energetic redoublings of human efforts at mastering our fate and finding the origins in order to secure the future (one need think only of the recent Human Genome Project or the heated debates regarding genetic manipulation, cloning and genetically modified organisms to see that our hopes are still high, and that we are still charmed and disturbed by these images and the prospects they portend [Jardine, in press]).

"There Are Children All Around Us"

After even a cursory look at the intellectual atmosphere into which Jean Piaget was born, the name of one of his major works resonates: *The Origins of Intelligence in Children* (1952). As we shall now examine, his work draws heavily upon this rich intellectual atmosphere of recapitulation, progress and the search for origins.

In 1973, Richard Evans did a wonderful series of interviews with Piaget. One exchange in the middle

of these interviews betrays Piaget's influences:

EVANS: You stated that you were most fundamentally interested in the matter of how primitive man began to think, how knowledge evolves and that you became interested in cognitive development in children because this was the only way available of looking at the whole historical development of cognitive processes in man in general. Is this still your fundamental interest?

PIAGET: Yes. Of course that is quite right. My problem is the development of knowledge in general. Unfortunately, this history is very incomplete—especially at its primitive beginnings. So I am doing what biologists do when they cannot constitute a phylogenetic series, they study ontogenesis. (Piaget & Evans, 1973, p. 48)

This brief passage lays out two interrelated themes that form the heart of Jean Piaget's life work.

The first is this: Piaget was not interested in developing a general **epistemology**. True to his intellectual ancestry, he was interested in developing a **genetic epistemology**. What this means is quite simple. Epistemology, a branch of philosophy, with which Piaget often flirted over the course of his life, is concerned with the question, "What is knowledge?" Genetic epistemology is concerned with the question, "How does knowledge grow?" (Piaget, 1970a, p. 731).

Now in order to answer the question of how knowledge grows one would have to understand first of all what knowledge *is*—what *is* this "thing" whose growth we wish to study? We seem to be right back at epistemology. Piaget does not take this turn. He believed that the question of what knowledge is was a strictly philosophical question in which he had no interest. Instead, he turns to the sciences (logic, mathematics, biology, psychology, physics) for his definition of knowledge. Knowledge *as practised and understood by the sciences* is the object of Piaget's search for genetic origins. He is blunt about this

---

Epistemology

A branch of philosophy concerned with the nature (*logos*) of knowledge (*episteme*) that asks, "What is knowledge?"

Genetic epistemology

Piaget's term for his study of the origins of knowledge in the life of the child; this study asks, "How does knowledge grow?"

point and its limitations: "We agree to take as our system of reference, nature as science describes her. The choice of this system of reference is a convention, but we make use of this convention quite consciously" (Piaget, 1972b, p. 282).

Like many ventures in the late nineteenth and early twentieth centuries, Piaget begins with a feature of contemporary life—in his case, "the concepts and categories [and methods] of established science" (Inhelder, 1969, p. 23)—and asks after the origins of this establishment. His work is dedicated to providing what he calls an "indispensable genetic dimension" (Piaget, 1967, p. 116) to our understanding of the sciences and the knowledge to which those sciences pretend.

Here a second theme emerges, and a second ancestry as well. Jean Piaget's "fundamental interest" is in the development, the "genesis," of knowledge itself and its slow and sometimes troubled emergence in our species. His prime interest is phylogenetic: the sequence of development of knowledge in the human species, in its whole span from "its primitive beginnings" to the eventual emergence of the abstract disciplines of the sciences, especially logic and mathematics, and the rise of modern science, modern rationalism. Ideally, with such an interest,

> [T]he most fruitful, most obvious field of study would be reconstituting human history—the history of human thinking since prehistoric man. Unfortunately, we are not very well informed about the psychology of Neanderthal man. Since this field is not available to us, we shall do as biologists do [and such as Ernest Haeckel suggested] and turn to ontogenesis. Nothing could be more accessible to study than the ontogenesis of these notions. There are children all around us. (Piaget, 1971a, p. 13)

Jean Piaget is not interested in the "children all around us" and their development of knowledge for their own sake, but because children present the means and opportunity to explore *phylogenetic* development of knowledge. In the growth and development of the child, Piaget hopes to find an ontogenetic recapitulation of the phylogenetic emergence of the

concepts and categories of established science over the course of the history of the human species. As two commentators on Jean Piaget's work suggest, "the child is the real primitive among us, the missing link between prehistorical men and contemporary adults (Voneche & Bovet, 1982, 88).

Suddenly we are on peculiar ground as educators. Jean Piaget, who had a profound effect on education, does not have children and their development as his "fundamental interest." Rather:

> Research work in genetic epistemology seeks to analyse the mechanisms of the growth of knowledge insofar as it pertains to scientific thought and to discover the passages from states of least knowledge to those of the most advanced knowledge. To this end, the concepts and categories of established science such as those of space, time, causality, number, and logical classes, have been studied as they develop in the life of the child. (Inhelder, 1969, p. 23)

But again, the use of this phrase, "in the life of the child," should not mislead us into confusing Piaget's work with some form of child psychology. The latter is concerned with "the child for his own sake" (Piaget & Inhelder, 1969, viii), "the child himself" (Piaget, 1973, v). Genetic epistemology, on the other hand, "has as its object the examination of the formation of knowledge itself" (Piaget, 1973, v). And yet despite this slightly different "fundamental interest" from our own as educators, Jean Piaget's work is still full of compelling insights into children and how they experience the world. It brims with ideas about development, about primitive and mythological thinking, and about play, dreams and imagination.

What Follows

In the next chapter, we'll discuss one specific ancestor of Jean Piaget's work, the German Enlightenment philosopher Immanuel Kant. In 1767, Kant set forth an image of knowledge and how it operates that profoundly affected Piaget's work and served as a key precursor to what has become a prevailing educational philosophy, constructivism. By working our way through this Kantian ancestry, we see the incredible breakthrough of Jean Piaget's own work and how it models itself on and deviates from Kant's work.

Chapter 3 lays out Piaget's understanding of knowledge and its development. Concepts such as assimilation, accommodation, equilibration, stages, schema(ta), operations, as well as Piaget's characterizations of developmental stages of knowledge, from earliest infancy to the mastery of logico-mathematical knowledge, are outlined.

Since the abstract structure of Piaget's theory of development can easily appear very arcane and very distant from the lives of children and teachers, the life of the classroom, chapter 4 is made up of what could be called "Piagetian vignettes." These are stories, incidents, scenarios and lessons learned from the work of Jean Piaget.

Finally, chapter 5 makes some cautionary notes on the legacy of Jean Piaget's work. These cautionary notes are not at all meant to dissuade readers from an interest in Piaget. On the contrary, they are meant to continue the work of unearthing ancestries. Piaget's images of knowledge and how it operates, of children and their lives, are a great gift to us, but they also have unintended, often unimagined consequences. We will sketch some of these pedagogical, ecological and sociopolitical effects.

GLOSSARY

Epistemology—a branch of philosophy concerned with the nature (logos) of knowledge (episteme) that asks, "What is knowledge?"

Genetic epistemology—Jean Piaget's term to distinguish his own work on the genesis of knowledge in the life of the child from general epistemology. Piaget takes as his standard for "knowledge" its operation in the established sciences of the day and asks, "How does knowledge grow?"

Ontogeny—literally, the genesis, growth or development of the individual.

Phylogeny—literally, the genesis, growth or development of the species.

Recapitulation—a commonly held belief that the growth or development of the individual goes through the same stages as the growth or development of the species. The individual thus recapitulates the history of the species: ontogeny recapitulates phylogeny. Thus, to understand the development of one (the species), one can study the other (the individual).

Schema/schemata (plural)—Piaget's term to indicate a structure, category or organization of thought or action.

CHAPTER TWO

On the Origins of Constructivism

The Kantian Ancestry of Jean Piaget's Genetic Epistemology

In a recent undergraduate seminar, I held three pieces of white chalk in my hand and asked student-teachers to name properties of this object. Their answers came easily: white, dusty, brittle, round, solid, dry and so on. I wrote these on the board.

I then pointed to my open palm and asked, "How many pieces of chalk do I have in my hand?"

"Three," someone called out, and I added that to our list.

We used this simple, almost trivial exercise to help us understand and interpret a powerful and puzzling passage from David Elkind (1967, xii), one of Jean Piaget's most articulate interpreters: "Once a concept is constructed, it is immediately experienced so that it appears to the subject as a perceptually given property of the object and independent of the subject's own mental activity."

Properties of the Object

Using Elkind as a guide, we looked back at the white chalk and the easy conversation we'd had, and

the equally easy list we had made. In order to "immediately experience" the whiteness of the chalk as a "property of the object," we had used not just our eyes, but also a concept we'd all learned (in English, "white") as a way to communicate our experience to others. We then discussed how this property of chalk—its whiteness—is not a property of chalk alone. It is also a more general concept (a color) that is also the property of many other objects (clouds, this page you are reading, and so on). As one student-teacher put it so brilliantly:

"'White' isn't stuck to the chalk."

Another student-teacher said, with equal metaphorical brilliance:

"It floats above things."

Both of these students were invoking, knowingly or not, all sorts of old mythologies and images about ideas and concepts being "above us," housed not on Earth, but in the heavens.

Our judgement of "brittle" required something more kinaesthetic: hitting the chalk against the desk or remembering what happens when you accidentally drop a piece or snap it between your fingers, and so on. We pondered the fact that, as adults, we can simply recall—or imagine—ourselves or someone else having snapped the chalk in the past. This judgement about the "brittleness" of chalk is almost ancient in our individual life-experiences. We've all experienced the brittleness of chalk in a myriad of ways in our lives as well as the analogue of its brittleness in a china cup or a terracotta flowerpot. The lived history of the slow construction, consolidation and reconstruction of this experience—all this "mental activity" as Elkind calls it, and more—of the brittleness of chalk in each of our lives is astoundingly complex and virtually untraceable.

In all of the words from our list, what appeared at first to be simple, obvious properties of the object gave way to a myriad of actual, possible or remembered actions, experiences, sensations, concepts, images, names and fantasies. These actions involved mental activity, but also involved the eyes, the hands, the body and all its housed memories and images of previous experiences. According to Piaget, these seemingly straightforward properties of the object are so familiar to adults that we have lost track of the fact that we had, in each case, to *construct* this familiarity over time. Whiteness, then, is not merely a property of the object, but more difficultly, a property of *the relationship(s)* between the object and the sense-making activities of the person experiencing the object. These sense-making activities are deeply ingrained, almost automatic and numerous in kind: bodily, ideational, imaginative, conceptual, logical, cultural, linguistic, biographical, historical/generational, perceptual, numerical, kinaesthetic, playful and so on.

According to Piaget, simply pointing to the object and asserting that it is white is both commonsensical and also, in some sense, naive and unreflective of the nature of knowledge and the profoundly active role that the human being takes in the act of knowing that yes, this chalk is white. Similarly, in speaking with a young child about how many pieces of chalk I have in my hand, it is commonsensical to believe that I *really do* have three pieces; if the child doesn't understand this, the problem is in the child, not in reality. Jean Piaget pushes this commonsense to the point of breaking. On the contrary, he argues, for the young child who cannot understand counting, enumerating, adding up, the world *does not have,* "in reality," a "number" of things, except perhaps "lots" and "none" and "more" and so on. In the presence of a very young child, I do not straightforwardly have three pieces of chalk in my hand because this child does not know how to "do" enumeration. His or her world is not enumerated; it is not constructed, thought of, understood or acted upon in that manner. I know how to enumerate and find numbers commonplace in the world as I experience and understand it, but I know this action so well that I might falsely believe that "three" is a property of the object, rather than a function of my experience and understanding—experience and understanding that the non-numerate child does not share.

Further, since we do not share experience and understanding, it is not just our adult psychological makeups, interior states or conceptual frameworks that differ from children. Since the terms we use to construct the world are different, our *worlds* are different. Hence, from the legacy of constructivism and Piagetian theory, we can sensibly speak these days about "the world of the child" and have it mean something quite disturbing, something quite profound that threatens to interrupt our self-confident ascription of properties to objects. It is the beginning of a self-consciousness regarding just who we mean by "we" and "our."

This is, in part, what Piaget learned from his work with children and with his attempts to standardize Binet's intelligence tests in light of adult standards of knowing: typically, children seemed to put things together differently than adults. As adults, we have learned these standards so well that we tend to "forget" our long and complex agency in the world we experience. We come to think it's all just "the way things really are," forgetting that we have, collectively and individually, *learned* "the way things really are" by collectively and individually *making something* of our experiences.

As can be imagined, my student teachers were not especially happy with this exercise. When we start disrupting seemingly obvious, commonplace things, the first response is often confusion, speechlessness, sometimes frustration and anger. These responses are important: once we have constructed our knowledge of a simple object like white chalk, that construction immediately and automatically appears to be a property of the object. Our constructions, that is, are *objectified*. This process is so deeply ingrained, so deeply buried, that unearthing it can feel humiliating, like a sort of betrayal. In these responses, we see the beginning of an awareness of our ongoing, unintended, often unconscious implication in what we know.

Much more pointed pedagogical consequences also occurred in this incident. One student talked of

seeing a teacher hovering over a young child and saying, "Just *look,* would you? Pay attention. There are *six* pictures on the worksheet. *See?*" In this story and others we all got a glimpse of how often we have treated th*e outcomes* of our own constructions as if they are absolute properties of the object, becoming frustrated by those who do not understand what is so obvious to any adult.

All of this illustrates a profound idea that underwrites Jean Piaget's work, an idea that has gained great power and, ironically, sometimes even greater obscurity in educational theory and practice: **constructivism**.

This is not the place to unravel all of the current threads of that phenomenon. Rather, we need to explore another thread in the intellectual atmosphere out of which Jean Piaget's work emerged. In the late 19th and early 20th century in European academic life, an historical figure rose to new prominence, from whom Piaget inherited these images of knowledge as construction: Immanuel Kant (1724–1804).

Immanuel Kant's contribution to the work of Jean Piaget is incredibly important, especially in light of a terrible dilemma that arises if we push this insight regarding constructivism too hard. The dilemma is this: given our differing backgrounds, languages, cultures, constructions, assumptions and experience, it would seem that our knowledge, experience and understanding of the world should be scattershot, too. It would appear that each of us brings only difference and diversity to the act of knowing. Knowledge consequently appears always and only personal; to use the old Greek distinction, knowledge is always and only mere opinion. It would seem, if we push this insight of constructivism too far, that each of us is locked into our own individual "bubble" and that any attempt to escape would only confirm our situation—attempting to understand another person's world would only be an act of *constructing* that other person and their world in light of my own framework. This is a

Constructivism

The idea that we actively construct our ongoing experience and understanding of the world based on previously acquired categories, concepts and experiences.

teacher's horror: What if I have imposed my own presumptions, prejudices, constructs and assumptions on a student?

Immanuel Kant brings to this dilemma, and Jean Piaget carries forward, what could be called an Enlightenment ideal: the belief that underlying our myriad backgrounds, languages, cultures, constructions, assumptions, and experiences are commonly held categories, forms or methods of knowledge: commonly held ways of constructing knowledge and objectivity, commonly held ways in which human reason essentially operates. Despite all our accidental differences and idiosyncracies adult human reason is, in limited and specific ways, always and everywhere the same in its judgements about objects in the world. It is the great task, both in the work of Immanuel Kant and in the world of Jean Piaget, of discovering this universal and necessary—happening in all cases (universal) and happening of necessity and not just by chance (necessary)—character of human reason.

Even though Kant and Piaget share an understanding of knowledge as construction, what each of them claims as universal and necessary to these constructions differs. The rest of this chapter contains a detailed look at how Immanuel Kant took up this task of understanding the universal and necessary character of human reason. This will help us understand both a defining source of Jean Piaget's work (and hence a defining source of educational theory and practice) as well as how Piaget's work departs from that source.

Kant's "Copernican Revolution"

> One can feel very close to the spirit of Kantianism (and I believe I am close to it). (Piaget, 1965a, p. 57)

Immanuel Kant's so-called **Copernican Revolution** in philosophy reclaimed at the epistemological level what was lost at the cosmological level in the work of Nicolaus Copernicus (1473–1543). In astronomy, Copernicus had overturned the belief that the Earth was the centre of creation, placing the

Copernican Revolution

Kant's ironic term to describe his repositioning of the human individual—as a knowing, meaning-constructing subject—at the centre of the knowable universe, despite Copernicus's conclusion that the sun, not Earth, lies at the physical center of the universe.

sun at the centre of the physical universe instead. Obviously, this original Copernican Revolution had consequences far beyond astronomy. By unseating Earth from its special cosmological place, humanity itself was de-centred.

Immanuel Kant reclaimed the centrality of humanity by putting human reason and its structures and characteristics at the centre of the knowable universe. Anything "knowable" refers back to the conditions of knowability determined by the essential, constructive character of human reason. But there is an extra step to watch for in this reclaiming of the centre. According to Kant, human reason, by its very nature, puts things together in clearly definable ways. It is an actively organizing, ordering, constructive human faculty, not a passive one. It is, as Kant defined it, a *synthesizing* faculty that, in the act of knowing something in the world, actively constructs orderliness out of the chaos of experience in accordance with human reason's own structures, forms and categories. Over a century later, Jean Piaget (1971c, xii) would call this "imposing cosmos on the chaos of experience."

To be an object in the world, according to Kant, means to have been constructed as an object according to human reason's criteria of "objectivity." To hearken back to the passage from David Elkind and our chalk lesson, we objectify our own constructions; we construct what it means for something to be an object in the world, and we experience the construction not just as mental activity of ourselves as subjects, but also as a property of the object. Human reason, in Kant's work, is thus not merely the centre of the knowable world of objects. It is also the centre of the construction and issuance of the order, structure and reason of that world. To hearken back to our simple example, the world has a number of things only because I am "numerate" and construct the world accordingly, demanding that it answer my questions regarding its number.

Immanuel Kant lays out this theory of knowledge or epistemology in his brilliant and difficult work

Critique of Pure Reason (originally published in 1787). It is this "spirit of Kantianism" (Piaget, 1965a, p. 57) and its legacies that filled the intellectual atmosphere of Jean Piaget's own thinking. As stated in the preface to Kant's text:

> A light broke upon the students of nature. They learned that reason has insight only into that which it produces after a plan of its own, and that it must not allow itself to be kept, as it were, in nature's leading-strings, but must itself show the way with principles of judgement based on fixed laws, constraining nature to give answer to questions of reason's own determining. Reason . . . must approach nature in order to be taught by it. It must not, however, do so in the character of a pupil who listens to everything the teacher chooses to say, but of an appointed judge who compels the witnesses to answer questions which he had himself formulated. While reason must seek in nature, not fictitiously ascribe to it, whatever has to be learnt, if learnt at all, only from nature, it must adopt as its guide, in so seeking, that which it has itself put into nature. (Kant, 1964, p. 20)

Unique here and of especial interest to educators is this new element: conceiving of knowledge as an active, constructive, orderly and ordering, *demand* made upon things. "To know," henceforth, is no longer understood as passively receiving information from an object (think of all those old "filling an empty vessel" images of education, or ones of "writing on a blank tablet," the **tabula rasa**).

Rather, "to know" is "to impose structure," "to (give) order(s)," "to demand," "to determine," "to make." To know is to *act,* in definable, determinable ways. Kant's work stands at the advent of what has come to be known as constructivism. By examining some of the steps Kant takes in building this image of human reason as an active, ordering, constructive faculty, we'll get a better picture of exactly how Piaget took up this challenge in his own work and transformed it radically in his own genetic epistemology.

Tabula rasa

The theory that the mind is a passive blank slate, written on by experience. Piaget and Kant do not accept this theory.

Two Types of Knowledge:
A Posteriori and *A Priori*

Empiricism

The theory that all knowledge is derived from perceptual (empirical) experience and thus leads only to increasingly probable generalizations about objects rather than universal and necessary knowledge. Piaget and Kant disagree with this.

One central argument in Kant's *Critique of Pure Reason* is that **empiricism** does not provide an adequate account of all forms of knowledge. In the theory of knowledge called empiricism, the human mind begins as a blank slate upon which are written the results of empirical, perceptual experience, which forms the basis of all knowledge. All knowledge of objects, therefore, is passively received from objects through the senses. To use the language of David Hume (1711–1776), a central empiricist philosopher, we know what something is because that thing and its characteristics *impress themselves* upon us. Empiricism (from the Greek *empeiria*, "experience," as opposed to *eidos* and *theoria*, ideas and theories) does not deny that humans act upon impressions received through the senses. However, the only sort of human action that can lead to any sort of knowledge, according to empiricism, is an action that occurs *after* this initial "receiving," that is, *posterior* to it. Simply put, all knowledge, for empricism, is a generalization following from and based upon experience. This is what Kant calls **a posteriori knowledge**.

A posteriori knowledge

knowledge that is acquired only after sensory or perceptual experience. Kant considered this knowledge particular but not universal or necessary.

According to empiricism, the only warrantable action upon experience is a generalization based upon and limited to the instances of experience. Such generalizations are always subject to the continuing influx of experiences, which may in the next instance prove a generalization incorrect. Hence the conclusions drawn from experience are not universal, necessary or binding, but only general(ized), contingent and dependent upon the next instance. To return to the example of the white chalk: knowing that it is chalk and that it is white can only be understood and judged *after* we have experienced the chalk and seen, over and over, that it is white. Moreover, if we had only ever experienced white chalk and we acted upon that knowledge to suggest that "all chalk is white," we would have generalized those experiences into a false statement. Not all chalk is white.

Even with the chalk in our example, empiricism strictly suggests that we cannot say absolutely and necessarily that it is white—or even that it is chalk! We can only say that based upon the past instances we have observed, we judge it to be white chalk, and it is most probable that it will be experienced as white chalk in the future. The more times we experience the chalk, the more probable our judgement becomes (in modern science, it is left to the science of statistics to determine degrees of probability). However, empiricism demands that it is always at least *possible* that future experiences will contradict this judgement, and that it may have to be revised. Empirical judgements are never universal and necessary. They are always only probable and subject to revision. This way of proceeding is, of course, central to the natural sciences. We experience things, we generalize, but those generalizations are always subject to what new experiences might bring. To put a finer point on this, David Hume suggested that the generalizations we make cannot be traced back to a single incident that gave rise to them, since the generalization was not impressed upon the senses by experience, but was, rather, produced by the mind (by what Hume called "association"). Such products of the mind are not, so to speak, "properties of the object" but are only ideas that have no definitive objective reality.

Immanuel Kant's work began elsewhere. He began by affirming the de facto existence of logic, mathematics and Euclidean geometry as forms of knowledge that are precisely *not* empirical generalizations. He argued that there is, in these sciences, another type of knowledge that is not derived from experience (*a posteriori*) but rather is imposed upon experience with a universality and a necessity—with a certainty, we should add—for which empiricism cannot give an adequate account.

Kant maintained that the universality and necessity of logic and mathematics (disciplines that, as we shall see, are central to Jean Piaget's genetic epistemology) were an indication that a type of knowledge

A priori knowledge

knowledge possessed *prior to* and independently of sensory or perceptual experience. Kant considered this knowledge universal and necessary.

Formal logic

A branch of philosophy concerned with the formal ways in which thoughts or statements are logically related.

Table of Judgements

Kant's table of the formal, logical ways in which one thought (necessarily and universally) relates to and can be synthesized with another thought.

exists that is not *a posteriori,* but rather **a priori knowledge**.

We have *a priori* knowledge of objects *prior to* and independently of empirical experience. Kant maintains (as does Jean Piaget) that when we make the judgement "the chalk is white," not all of this knowledge comes from experiencing the chalk. Some of this knowledge—its general, universal and necessary structure—is known prior to and independently of experiencing the chalk. That is to say, even if I kept my hand closed, and the students in the class had no idea what particular object was in my hand, they would still be able to have some general knowledge of that object.

On the face of it, this sounds very odd. Here are the steps that Immanuel Kant took in making his case, and some of the consequences that follow from it.

Kant began with an age-old philosophical discipline: **formal logic**. Formal logic delineates the essential, *a priori* (that is, universal and necessary) interrelations between one thought and another. It describes what Jean Piaget (1952, p. 15) called "the organization of thought itself." It is, so to speak, the grammar of thinking, its structure and forms. In formal logic, we have a whole array of formal judgements that can be made. This list of formal judgements extends back in Western thought as far as the work of Aristotle (circa 300 B.C.E.). In the *Critique of Pure Reason,* Kant lists these formal judgements in what he calls the **Table of Judgements** (see Kant, 1964, p. 107 and following). Formal logic, however, only describes the ways in which one thought might formally, logically relate to another. Here are three simple examples of isolated logical judgements:

A is A
A is B
If A, then B.

These statements seem quite abstract and empty until we see what Kant does with his Table of Judgements. The brilliance of Kant's work lies in his suggestion that since these forms of thinking are

the universal and necessary forms we always and unavoidably use to think about an object in the world, they thus *prescribe* what we think about that object (at least in general terms). These forms of thinking give shape to our perceptual, empirical experiences and turn our perceptions into objects. They are the forms, therefore, not only of thinking, but of objectivity itself—they are the forms that an object of knowledge must necessarily and universally take, since they are the forms that prescribe how that object is constructed out of perceptions.

In this limited sense, then, we do have knowledge of objects in the world that is not *derived from* our perceptual experience of those objects but rather is a set of demands made by thinking upon perceptual experience; the nature of thinking itself is a demand that forms our perceptual experiences into objects. These formative, constructive demands made upon objects in the world do not therefore constitute a merely formal logic, which simply describes forms of thinking. These formative, constructive demands made upon objects in the world constitute what Immanuel Kant called **transcendental logic**.

That is, these unavoidable, universal and necessary, formative, constructive demands provide the logic whereby the human subject transcends itself and actively *forms* objects according to its own constructions, its own demands, its own "mental activity" (Elkind, 1967, xii). Transcendental logic thus describes the universal and necessary logic of objectivity itself, the logic of the knowable world that the structure of human reason has itself constructed according to its own demands.

This is a difficult idea. It will become a little less murky if we list some of these formal/logical forms of thought and see how, in each case, they might apply to our knowledge of the white pieces of chalk.

First (and, for many philosophers and mathematicians, most fundamental) is the formal, logical judgement of identity: A = A. Although this seems arcane, it is actually quite simple and very important. When you work with a formula (both in logic and math-

Transcendental logic
Kant's term for logic wherein the subject's logical forms of thinking make formative, constructive demands upon perceptual experiences to shape them into objects.

ematics), each time you run into the term "a," it is always the same "a." Even if "a" is as yet undefined (as, for example, in the equation $2a + b = b-a$), we know, we presume, the logic of human thinking *demands* that in both its appearances in this equation, $a = a$, and likewise, in both its appearances, $b = b$.

When it functions transcendentally and not just logically, this so-called principle of identity becomes one of the universal and necessary ways that we define and construct what it means to be an object in the world: whatever an object might be, our thinking demands that it is what it is, and it isn't something else. Consider this: even when my hand is closed around those three pieces of white chalk and the students cannot see what the object is, they *already know* that, whatever it is, it is what it is. It is a self-identical thing. Kant borrowed this age-old principle from the work of Aristotle. Consider, from his *Metaphysics:*

> Not to have one meaning is to have no meaning and if words have no meaning, our reasoning with one another, and indeed with ourselves has been annihilated; for it is impossible to think of anything if we do not think of one thing. (Aristotle, Book IV)

We know, independently of our empirical experience of an object (which yields *a posteriori* knowledge), that the object is self-identical, because it is impossible, it is contradictory, it is unreasonable, to think otherwise of things. This is *a priori* knowledge.

Those student-teachers in our example also know a myriad of other things in this *a priori* way: the object in my hand, whatever it is, is a thing which has properties ("A is B," even if we don't know what defines A or B in this particular case); it exists in time and has spatial, geometrical characteristics (to use Kantian terms, space and time are the *a priori* forms of perception, such that even our empirical experience has its own *a priori* forms—this accounts for the *a priori*, universal and necessary character of Euclidean geometry); it is numerable and measurable; it was created or caused by something or other (from the logical judgement "If A, then B," we get the transcenden-

tal judgement, "All objects have a cause"); and so on. These things are, in general, and universally and necessarily, what it means to be an object in the world. If we hear a knock at the door, we know that it has a cause, even if we don't yet know *what* the cause is. It is unreasonable to think, for example, that the knock was not caused by anything. It must be someone at the door, or something falling against the door, or some other noise that I mistook for a knock, or an illusion. We cannot reasonably believe that it was caused by nothing at all, that it just happened. That is, so to speak, *unthinkable*. Things in the knowable, objective world don't just happen—they are *caused*.

This bears repeating regarding our example of white chalk. To know that *what* is in my hand is three pieces of white chalk requires empirical experience. To this extent, empiricism is correct, and the knowledge to be had is *a posteriori*. However, to know that it is something self-identical, that it has properties, that it exists in space in measurable ways, that it is a thing that was caused by other things in the world does *not* require empirical experience. To this extent, empiricism is not an adequate account, because this knowledge is had *a priori* and is not a probable generalization but rather universal and necessary.

Here is where Kantian theory (and, following it, Piagetian theory) becomes profound in its consequences and effects. The *a priori* knowledge that my students have of the pieces of chalk in my hand is a knowledge, not just of this chalk, but of *any possible object of knowledge*. It is universal and necessary knowledge about what Kant calls "an object in general." It is now possible to understand what might have originally been a quite contentious assertion: "the *a priori* conditions of a possible experience in general are at the same time conditions of the possibility of objects of experience" (Kant, 1964, p. 138). Or, differently put, "the most the understanding can achieve *a priori* is to anticipate the form of a possible experience in general" (Kant, 1964, p. 264).

A Final Thread of the Kantian Legacy

> The order and regularity in [what] we call *nature,* we ourselves introduce. We could never find [such orderliness and regularity] . . . had not we ourselves, or the nature of our mind, originally set them there. (Kant, 1964, p. 147)

This is starting to sound rather bizarre—the orderliness of the world is our construction? Again:

> [Human] understanding is itself the lawgiver of nature. Save through it, nature, that is, synthetic unity of the manifold of [perceptual] appearances according to rules [imposed by reason itself], should not exist at all. (Kant, 1964, p. 148)

At this juncture a great distinction arises that has troubled philosophers ever since Kant introduced it into philosophical discourse, a distinction between nature "in itself" and nature "for us." The latter sense of "nature for us" is what David Elkind was hinting at when he spoke about properties of the object which appear to be what the object *itself* is, but are, in fact, what the object is in relation to us and our thinking and acting. For example, when we experience "white" as a property of the object, what we are in fact experiencing is a relation between the object and our mental activity, which has constructed our perceptual experience according to its own categories and concepts. Kant suggests that the question, "What is this object as it exists *independently* of our constructions?" is absurd, because to ask such a question is to think and reason about this object and therefore, to place it back in relation to us and our thinking and reasoning. Thus Kant concludes:

> That nature should direct itself [in] conformity to law[s imposed by human reason], sounds very strange and absurd. But consider that this nature is not a thing in itself but is merely an aggregate of appearances, so many representations of the mind. (1964, p. 140)

And:

> The question arises how it can be conceivable that nature should have to proceed in accordance with categories which . . . are not derived from it, and

do not mold themselves on its pattern? The solution of this seeming enigma is as follows. Things in themselves would necessarily, apart from any understanding that knows them, conform to laws of their own. But appearances are only representations of things that are unknown as regards what they may be in themselves. As mere representations, they are subject to no law of connection save that which the connecting faculty prescribes. (Kant, 1964, p. 178)

Here lies the great breakthrough of Kantian theory and the great consequence of constructivism: objectivity in the sciences is not achieved by finding out what things "really" are in themselves but by following the rules of human reason, the very rules that define and determine the essential characteristics of objectivity in the first place. We always and only understand things by striking up a relation to them, a relation in which the human subject is not simply the passive recipient of information from the object but is an active agent in the formation of how the object can be experienced. Things that are in relation to us ("objects of experience and knowledge") are not things-in-themselves. To *know* something is to *put* it into relation with us. Things-as-known are not things-in-themselves. We can never know those things that might "conform to laws of their own." We can only know that which reason produces after a plan of its own. And we can know the universal and necessary characteristics of this plan. We can know the universal and necessary characteristics of the objective world.

To push this one more step, nature-in-itself may, in this epistemology, be preserved from the imposition of human reason, but in such preservation, it is rendered "unknowable" *by definition,* since to know nature is to place nature "under the sway" of human imposition. However, as a correlate to such preservation, the knowable world becomes a closed system that has reason as its master. Reason becomes answerable only to itself. It becomes, to use Piagetian terminology, "self-regulating" (Piaget, 1971b, p. 26).

Returning to the Question of Origins

> Accordingly, the spontaneity of understanding becomes the formative principle of receptive matter, and in one stroke we have the old mythology of an intellect which glues and rigs together the world's matter with its own forms. (Heidegger, 1985, p. 70)

In his search for the origins of human reason, Kant draws two conclusions:

1 The origin of human reason is found not in the chance outcomes of and generalizations from empirical experience, but in its universal and necessary *a priori* forms, its categories, its structures, its essential characteristics.

2 Human reason is a demand made upon the world, not unlike a judge compelling his witness to give answer to questions of "Reason's own determining" (Kant, 1964, p. 20). Reason is a giving of order(s), a construction, a making, a forming, a structuring, a categorizing, an organizing.

With Kant's image of the originary character of reason, we have what George Grant called "the wedding of knowing and production" (Grant, 1998, p. 1).

Jean Piaget, as we have noted, feels "close to the spirit of Kantianism," but it is difficult to see yet precisely how this could be. Piaget's work with young children and his work on the Simon-Binet intelligence tests taught him that what Kant takes to be the universal and necessary structures or categories of human reason are precisely *not* universal and necessary: they are not universally and necessarily shared by young children.

This dilemma proves to be the core of Jean Piaget's work: how is it that a squalling, totally dependent infant can, over the course of its life, come to master logic and mathematics in such a way that logic and mathematics appear (as they did to Kant) to be universal and necessary? Or, to put it more colloquially, "How, in reality, is science possible?" (Piaget, 1970a, p. 731). We turn next to Piaget's answer.

GLOSSARY

A priori knowledge—literally, a knowledge of objects of experience that is possessed *prior to* and independently of our sensory or perceptual experience of those objects. For example, prior to looking into the trunk of my car, I know ahead of time that, whatever object might be in the trunk exists in space and time, it is self-identical, it has a material cause, it has properties that can be ascribed to it. Kant considered *a priori* knowledge to be universal (it applies to any possible object of experience) and necessary (it is not contingent on further experience of the object).

A posteriori knowledge—literally, a knowledge of objects of experience that is possessed only *after* we have had sensory or perceptual experience of those objects. Kant considered *a posteriori* knowledge to be particular and in no way necessary. We need to open the trunk of my car to know, for example, that there is a tire-iron in it, that it is heavy, black, metal and so on.

Constructivism—this term can be loosely applied to Kant's epistemology and to Piaget's genetic epistemology. It means that, in our interactions with the world, we actively *construct* our experience and understanding in accord with the categories, concepts and previous experiences that we bring to the situation.

Copernican Revolution—Kant's term for his repositioning of the human subject at the centre of the knowable universe, in a reverse of the work of Copernicus (which placed the sun, rather than Earth, at the center of the physical universe). Kant placed the knowing subject at the centre of the knowable universe since the knowing subject demands that the things of the world live up to its own ways of knowing. As a constructive, synthesizing faculty, human reason constructs and synthesizes experiences into objects.

Empiricism—an epistemology that both Kant and Piaget argue against, empiricism says that all knowledge is derived from empirical or perceptual experience. All knowledge is thus *a posteriori* and leads not to any universal and necessary conclusions but only to empirical generalizations about objects.

Formal logic—a branch of philosophy concerned with the formal ways in which thoughts or statements are logically related to one another. For example, I can propose the formal/logical syllogism: "If A, then B." "A." "Therefore B." If we accept the first premise of this syllogism ("If A occurs, then B occurs") and we accept the second premise ("A has

occurred"), we are *logically compelled* to accept its conclusion ("B occurs"). This is *a formal requirement of thinking,* not a statement about *objects in the world.* Because of this, a syllogism can be logical (follow the rules of thinking) and yet false. For example, *if* we accept the following two premises—"If it rains, there must be fire in the sky" and "It rains"—we are *logically required* to accept the conclusion "There must be fire in the sky." This conclusion *follows logically* from the two premises, even though it is false.

Table of Judgements: Kant's Table of Judgements lists the formal, logical ways in which one thought necessarily and universally relates to and can be logically synthesized or brought together with another thought (see formal logic).

Tabula rasa—literally, "blank slate." A empirical theory of knowledge that suggests the human mind is a blank slate onto which the results of perceptual or sensory experience are inscribed. Thus, all knowledge is *a posteriori,* the outcome of experience. This concept also underwrites a common educational belief that someone can learn anything if the material is presented often enough and with enough reinforcement. Piaget and Kant both reject the mind as a tabula rasa. The mind, they believe, is not empty but rather holds a set of structured ways of knowing that make demands on empirical experience—that make demands, therefore, on what can be learned from experience.

Transcendental logic—Kant's term for the logic whereby the subject's logical forms of thinking (see formal logic) go beyond ("transcend") the mind to form objects of experience. It parallels the forms of thinking found in the Table of Judgements, but describes not the formal relation of one thought to another but rather the relation of those formal relations to objects. The forms of transcendental logic are detailed in Kant's Table of Categories.

CHAPTER THREE

Jean Piaget and the Origins of Intelligence

A Return to "Life Itself"

Affinity and Distance from "The Spirit of Kantianism"

> One can feel very close to the spirit of Kantianism (and I believe I am close to it). [However] the necessity characteristic of the syntheses [Kant's *a priori* categories of Reason are the universal and necessary ways that experience is "knit together" by Reason. They are "synthesizing." They are "syntheses"] becomes [in my work] a *terminus ad quem* and ceases to be [as in Immanuel Kant's work] a *terminus a quo*. (Piaget, 1965a, p. 57)

In this passage, Jean Piaget articulates both his affinity to and his distance from the work of Immanuel Kant, which we shall examine briefly to illuminate Piaget's profound originality and contribution to educational theory and practice.

In Piaget's work, the universality and necessity of the categories of human reason articulated by Kant in his *Critique of Pure Reason* are not the starting point (*terminus a quo*) of human reason, but its end point (*terminus ad quem*). These categories

describe, Piaget argues, typical mature adult reasoning and are therefore not the origin of knowledge, but the outcome. They are not present from the beginning and/or present in each case but emergent over time.

In order to unpack the consequences of this insight for educational theory and practice, let's first elaborate on Kant's two conclusions from his search for the origins of human reason discussed in the previous chapter:

1   The origin (here understood in the sense of most basic, most essential, most "original") of human reason is found not in the chance outcomes of and generalizations from individual empirical experience but in its universal and necessary *a priori* forms, categories and structures: those definitive, unavoidable characteristics without which human reason would not be human reason.

2   Additionally, human reason's *a priori* forms, according to Kant, constitute a demand made upon the world. Human understanding is full of agency and determination. It is active, not passive. The ways that humanity *gives* orders are more "original," more fundamental, more basic, than the ways it *takes* orders. The former—the orders we give—*forms* what we take to be the order of the world. Thus, the categories of human reason shape or construct perceptual input into objects. To recall one of our examples: our *a priori* knowledge that the object in my hand is a self-identical thing ("A = A," whatever "A" might be), that it is a thing with properties ("A = B"), and that it has a cause ("If A, then B") is more basic than the particular *a posteriori* knowledge that this piece of chalk is white. The latter is empirical information we learn *from* experience; the former we *impose on* experience. The forms "A = A" and "A is B" and "If A, then B" (there are twelve such categories in the Kantian **Table of Categories**) are basic to any possible object, one particular example of which is the white chalk. To know

Table of Categories

Kant's Table of Categories parallels his Table of Judgements in structure but lists the ways in which the universal and necessary synthesizing functions of thinking construct and determine how we think about objects in the world (see transcendental logic).

that I have white chalk in my hand requires empirical experience. To know that I have a self-identical object with properties in my hand does not. Human reasoning is thus an orderly and ordering act of construction, of categorizing, of organizing and synthesizing.

In the passage cited at the beginning of this chapter, Piaget is saying that, although he feels close to the "spirit of Kantianism," the origin of human reason is *not* to be found in its *a priori* forms. In Piaget's work, these structures or categories—those that are characteristics of adult reasoning and that underwrite the disciplines of logic and mathematics—are not "originary." As he discovered in his work with the Simon-Binet intelligence tests and in his detailed conversations with children, those structures or categories:

- sequentially emerged over time, over the history of the species (phylogeny). The "concepts and categories [and methods] of established science"(Inhelder, 1969, p. 23) appear rather late in the history of the human species, and they
- sequentially re-emerge over a lifetime, over the history of the individual (ontogeny). The concepts, categories and methods of established science appear only as the person slowly reaches a certain cognitive maturity.

Since the concepts, categories and methods of established science emerge[d], they cannot be universal and necessary to the character of human intelligence. A newborn infant does not structure the world in these ways, even though, somehow, over the course of that child's development, he or she comes to be able to master logic and mathematics, disciplines fundamental in the Kantian categories. So, here is the rub for Piaget: how is it possible that something like the Kantian categories can be absent in the life of very young children, can develop over time and yet, in the end, can take on the character of universality and necessity in the disciplines of mathematics and logic? How is it possible that estab-

lished science can emerge out of the embodied, concrete, animistic, image-filled, playful life of a young child chasing and bursting bubbles?

Piaget's work shares this characteristic with Kant's: both argue that the "original" characteristic of human reason is that it is an active, organizing, structuring demand made upon the world. However, typical adult human reasoning (like the type tested for in the Simon-Binet intelligence tests), and its handmaiden disciplines, logic and mathematics, are only a late-arriving set of structures and ordering demands. However, they are a reflection of the fact that all of human life—from the frail actions of a newborn infant, to a child bursting bubbles and laughing, to those student teachers counting up pieces of white chalk, to the pristine and abstract intricacies of a mathematician's scrawls—has the character of such a demand:

> *Every relation* between the living being and its environment [not just those in logic and mathematics and the logic of objectivity characteristic of the concepts and categories and methods of established science] has this particular characteristic: the former, instead of submitting passively to the latter, modifies it by imposing on it a certain structure of its own. (Piaget, 1952, p. 118, emphasis added)

Piaget believes that there is a "self-organizing principle *inherent in life itself*" (1952, p. 19, emphasis added). Such order-giving activity is not exclusive, therefore, to logic and mathematics. This self-organizing principle inherent in life itself defines, for Jean Piaget, the origins of human intelligence.

Jean Piaget's Biological Vision of the Functional *A Priori*

Genetic epistemology is concerned with providing what Piaget maintains is an "indispensable genetic dimension" to our understanding of the concepts, categories and methods of established science, like those articulated by Kant. It is, as we have discussed, interested in the question, "How does

knowledge grow?" (Piaget, 1970a, p. 731). How is it that we, beginning as biological entities apparently possessed of only the simplest of reflexes, are "destined to master science" (Piaget, 1952, p. 372)?

In order to answer these sorts of perplexing questions, it is not enough for Piaget to locate human intelligence and the concepts and categories of established science as simple "relationship[s] among others between the organism and its environment" (Piaget, 1952, p. 19). Logic and mathematics do not just *accompany* the forms of structuring the world displayed by children or the biological functionings and structures of the human organism. The ability to understand logic and mathematics *originates in* and *emerges out of* the life of an organism that begins its days as a helpless infant.

In his *Origins of Intelligence in Children* (1952), Jean Piaget provides us with the clearest and most concise statement of his concerns in these matters, arguing that "from the fact that the living being achieves knowledge and that the child is one day destined to master science, we certainly believe that the conclusion must be drawn that there is a continuum between life and intelligence" (p. 372). Indeed, Piaget and his followers have provided us with a wealth of information that describes the structural differences "characteristic of each [developmental] level" (Piaget, 1952, p. 372) leading to the emergence of logic and mathematics. There are textbooks full of descriptions of the unique characteristics of Piaget's stages of cognitive development, and we will provide our own descriptions in the next chapter.

Piaget's work is also deeply concerned with the issue of "what is permanent in the course of this evolution" (1952, p. 372). In fact, "what is permanent" defines the order, sequence and characteristics of the stages of development. Therefore, the continuum underlying the slow genesis and emergence of the concepts and categories of established science is of great importance in understanding his stages of cognitive development and how they are sequenced and articulated in his work. Piaget believes a continuum

defines the slow emergence of knowledge in children, a sense of direction and organization; it is *not* simply the random accruing of empirical experience. Here is Piaget's great challenge to behaviourist theory. Children don't just *change* or modify behaviour in response to the whims of experience and stimuli, Piaget argues. Rather, he suggests, they *develop* in ways that have pattern, sequence and continuity.

What is the nature of this continuum? The title of the introductory chapter of *Origins of Intelligence in Children* immediately gives us a clue: "Biological Problem of Intelligence." Piaget writes:

> Intelligence is adaptation. In order to grasp its relation to life in general, it is necessary to state precisely the relations that exist between the organism and environment. Life is a continuous creation of increasingly complex forms and a progressive balancing of these forms with the environment. To say that intelligence is a particular instance of biological adaptation is thus to suppose that it is essentially an organization and that its function is to structure the universe just as the organism structures its environment. (1952, p. 4)

As we have already noted, according to Piaget, *all* interactions between the organism and the environment involve the living being modifying that environment "by imposing on it a certain structure of its own" (Piaget, 1952, p. 118).

Thus, one sense in which there is a universal and necessary continuity across development is that at no level of development can the environment be conceived as a ready-made organization that simply imposes itself on a passive organism-subject. Rather, the underlying organization of the organism, at any and all levels under consideration, actively structures the environment. Thus, once again in line with the "spirit of Kantianism," Piaget speaks against an empiricist conception of the nature of human intelligence that "tends to consider experience as imposing itself without the subject having to organize it" (Piaget, 1952, p. 362).

However, this sense of continuity alone does not yet account for the *emergence* of the concepts and

categories of established science in a way that is continuous with "life itself." There must be something about adaptation that leads to this emergence and that provides for this continuity. More fundamental—more "original"—than the varying structures of organism-environment interactions are the ways in which all of those structures *function.* All organism-environment interactions function in precisely the same manner. Piaget variously uses the terms "functional identity" (1952, p. 24), "functional analogy" (p. 237), or "**functional invariants.**"

These are assimilation, accomodation and equilibration, and they define the a priori character of any relationship between the organism and the environment. Rather than understanding the a priori as a set of structures (following Kant), Piaget believes that the a priori is functional in character and that the structures described by Kant are those that are best adapted to this invariant, universal and necessary functioning (pp. 8–13) and "functional correspondence" (1967, p. 3) to indicate that "the essential fact concerning this functioning is, in effect, absolute continuity" (Piaget, 1967, p. 141, emphasis added) across the wide array of structural or conceptual differences that define human developmental stages. "These functional analogies," Piaget clarifies, "do not at all imply an identity of structure" (1952, p. 240). The particular constructs differ and change over time—even those deemed a priori by Kant. However, despite such difference, "from the simplest of reflexes to the most systematic intelligence, the same method of operation seems to us to continue through all the stages, thus establishing a complete continuity between increasingly complex structures" (Piaget, 1952, p. 153, emphasis added). The newborn infant and the mathematician, it seems, function in exactly the same ways: even though their constructs of the world differ radically, how those constructs function remains continuous.

In Piaget's reworking of Kant, the functioning of life itself becomes what is *a priori,* and constructivism, a currently popular thread of educational

Functional invariants

Assimilation, accomodation and equilibration define the *a priori* character of *any* relationship between the organism and the environment.

theory and practice, is born (see Glossary, chapter 2).

Assimilation, Accommodation and Equilibration and the Pervasiveness of "Construction"

The terms that Piaget uses to describe this essentially continuous "method of operation" are assimilation, accommodation and equilibration.

Assimilation is the process whereby features of the environment are incorporated into the structure of the organism. It is a process of "integration into previous structures" (Piaget, 1967, p. 4)—what Immanuel Kant might call a "synthesizing act" (one that involves constructing, ordering, demanding, organizing, bringing together, linking). Thus, when those student teachers named the object I held "white chalk," they were not just passively receiving the input of a perceptual experience but rather were integrating and organizing that input by attempting to assimilate it into "previous structures" (previous organizations of thinking, previous concepts, categories, types, etc.). But note a subtle shift here that once again distances Piaget's work from that of Kant. This "integration into previous structures" is not only an integration into general, abstract structures such as "A = A" (it is a self-identical object), or "A is B" (it is an object with properties), or "If A, then B" (it is an object with a physical, material cause). Even the tentative, empirically general knowledge that "chalk is brittle" is *itself* constructive and ordering in nature. What has occurred here is that the idea of "construction" has become pervasive: *all* interactions between the organism and the environment are "constructive" and "organizing" and "ordering."

This idea has become so commonplace in our contemporary world, especially in the language and thinking of education, that it is difficult to fully experience the profundity of its arrival. To review: even empirically derived concepts—concepts derived from empirically experiencing chalk over the course of time—are ordering and constructive of future experiences. Simply put, because I have experienced chalk dozens of times over the course of my life, when

---

Assimilation

The functional process whereby the organism takes in and structures environmental stimuli according to a schema that defines what inputs will be allowed and how they will be organized.

I walk into a new and unfamiliar classroom, that chalk on the board's ledge is experienced by me as brittle because I construct my new experience of this new classroom in light of my previous experiences. Or, to use Piaget's terminology, I assimilate these new experiences to my previous assimilatory schemata or structures. This is how my previous experiences *function*—as ways of ordering my experience of this new classroom into a somewhat familiar place, as ways of "assimilating" this experience. The structuring, assimilating action of my previous experiences thus tends to stabilize my experience of the world. I don't have to constantly experience the immediacy and particularity of every moment. Because my assimilatory schemata provide order to the here-and-now of experience—"the *hic* and *nunc*" (Piaget, 1973 p. 9)—they buffer me from the constant newness of experience. The significance of this point is dual for educators:

- children are functioning in precisely this way— assimilating experience in the classroom in accord with their own "structures" or "schemata"—and, most disturbingly for beginning teachers,
- the previous experiences and order(s) that they bring to the classroom are not identical to those of a typical adult.

Assimilation is not just a cognitive matter or a cognitive function. The same functioning is at work, for example, in my digestion system. Calling something "edible" does not describe, to use David Elkind's phrase, a "property of the object." Rather, it describes the *relation between* my digestive system's "assimilatory structures" and the object. "Edibility," to use the Kantian terminology, is a demand made upon things, a "requirement" of the organism, not just a property of the object. The object is experienced as something edible because it can be integrated into the structures of my digestive system. If it couldn't be thus integrated—assimilated to an already existing structure—it wouldn't be edible. And, as we all know, if I attempt to assimilate it and I do not have the

assimilatory structures available to do so, I will, excuse me, "reject" it—in a rather visceral manner.

The brilliance of Piaget's understanding of cognitive development becomes clear as we pursue this line of thought. A young child who does not have the assimilatory schemata or structures that would allow her to "take in" (assimilate into already existing structures) information about, say, place-value in mathematics, will not be able to "understand" (assimilate into already existing structures) certain aspects of a classroom conversation—not because she isn't paying attention, but because her own structures of understanding do not allow for attention to be paid to this idea. So what happens? She'll ignore or reject the conversation altogether, push back against its incomprehensibility (a sort of cognitive "throwing up"), or she will take it in as best she can, given the structures of understanding she has available.

Here is a simple example from a second-grade child: "Twenty plus two is forty because two plus two is four and zero isn't worth anything." This is a perfect example of how the urge to assimilate is indigenous to our nature. Faced with an example like "20 + 2 =__?," *all of us*—adults and children alike, even the newborn infant—will bring to bear the structures we have available to assimilate this question and respond to it. Jean Piaget's work provides teachers sensitive to children and their efforts at understanding an opening: "40" is no longer simply incorrect. It is also a wonderful, necessary clue to understanding how this child is thinking, what structures and understandings this child is currently using, and, best of all, what concepts, structures and understandings are necessary for this child to grasp the idea of place-value and how it functions in our mathematics system.

The other essential feature of this method of operation is the process of **accommodation**. Clearly, the function of assimilation doesn't yet account for the fact that we learn and change over time, that the structures to which we assimilate our life-experiences grow and develop. Accommodation refers to

Accommodation

The functional process whereby the pre-existing schemta for structuring experience must adapt to new environmental input in order to return the organism-environment relationship to equilibrium.

the fact that the organism is often incapable of assimilating all elements of the environment into "previous structures." Over the course of development, new elements in the environment "cause the old framework to crack" (Piaget, 1971a, p. 397) and require the previous assimilatory structures to modify themselves to accommodate these new experiences.

The process of accommodation is the "result of pressures exerted by the environment" (Piaget, 1952, p. 6), but it does not function in the ways that behaviourism would suggest. To go back to our place-value example, when the child is confronted—slowly, carefully—with more and more examples of how the idea of place-value functions, her existing assimilatory schemata become systematically perturbed over time. She will begin to experience the fact that her current assimilatory schemata (more simply and commonsensically phrased, her current understandings of these matters) are not adequate to her environment and that something needs to be done. She needs to modify her understanding in order to accommodate new phenomena. If she does not, the pressures of the environment (a school life and a world in which numbers and issues of place-value inevitably exist) will be destabilizing. She needs, in short, to learn.

But "learning," here, is not a matter of simply accumulating more and more input, (as behaviourism would suggest), since the very conditions of her ability to *receive* input are at issue. In the face of these discrepant events, "learning" becomes a matter of modifying the terms of which input is possible—which input is demanded, organized, structured and "constructed." She does not learn the concept of place-value through repeated empirical instances (per the behavioural version of learning). Rather, she must *develop new structures,* new ways of assimilating, constructing and organizing the world. Granted, repeated external stimuli are a necessary condition for learning—they are necessary to the destabilization of previous assimilatory schemata—but they not a sufficient condition. An internal change is also necessary. If the new, discrepant experiences are too

severely different, the assimilatory structures will not change—neither will they change if the new, discrepant experiences are too familiar, since the new experiences will not disrupt or disturb the equilibrium of already existing structures.

Understanding this process has a profound effect on how we imagine our tasks as educators. First, development is not especially incremental. As many teachers have witnessed, sometimes children can be presented with repeated opportunities to learn a certain idea or task, but all to no avail—and then suddenly, a shift occurs, and what seemed impossible one day is commonplace the next. Those repeated opportunities have had a hand in this shift, but although the opportunities are incremental, the shift often is not. Sometimes we try to accelerate such shifts by presenting more frequent opportunities, with unreliable results. As the commonsense adage from Piaget's work warns, if children are not "developmentally ready," they cannot learn. All we can do is re-present the experiential opportunities, over and over, and patiently wait. Development takes time. As educators we must each realize this truth: just because I taught something several times, does not mean that students learned.

In the work of Jean Piaget, these functional invariants of assimilation and accommodation do not appear randomly in the life of the developing child. They are deeply rooted in a functioning of "life itself" that guides their appearance and, moreover, that guides the *direction* that development takes.

Equilibrium/equilibration

An organism strives to equilibrate, to achieve a balance or equilibrium, between accommodating and assimilating its environment.

Adaptation

An equilibrium between the organism and its environment, reached in increasingly inclusive and stable stages.

This deeper function, this deeper sense of continuity, is called **equilibrium**. "Equilibrium" is a term used to describe the relationship between assimilation and accommodation. "**Adaptation**," of which the concepts, categories and methods of established science are particular instances, "is an equilibrium between assimilation and accommodation" (Piaget, 1952, p. 6).

But here we've reached the same impasse. To say that the functions of assimilation, accommodation and equilibration are universally and necessarily

continuous across the different stages of development—all life is adaptation—still doesn't account for the unique *emergence* of the particular adaptations achieved in the concepts, categories and methods of established science. For Piaget, the concepts, categories and methods of established science are not simply one adaptation among others. Science is the end of adaptation, its fulfilment, its goal, its *terminus ad quem*. Human intelligence is, according to Piaget, "an *extension* and *perfection* of all adaptive processes" (Piaget, 1973, p. 7, emphasis original). Here we see traces of Piaget's intellectual ancestry in his profound belief that human reason and human intelligence, as manifest in established science, are the crowning moment of life itself. That adaptation, that way of constructing an understanding of the world, is the goal toward which life is moving, striving, developing (more on this and its consequences in chapter 5). For now, we have to figure out how this absolutely continuous functioning of adaptation (through assimilation, accommodation and equilibration) finds its "perfection" in the workings of established science.

"An All-Embracing Equilibrium" as the *Telos* of Development

Teleology/teleological
Seeking an end point (from the Greek *telos,* meaning "end" or "goal").

In Piaget's work, equilibrium is not a mere description of the relation between assimilation and accommodation. Equilibrium is also a **teleological** notion, and as such, it is an expression of "the fundamental reality about living things" (Piaget, 1967, p. 347). Development, in Piaget's understanding, can be characterized as a sequence of increasingly adaptive, increasingly equilibrated and stable plateaus or stages, each characterized by specifiable structures or schemata. In the middle of all these structural changes over time are the continuous and invariant functions of assimilation, accommodation and equilibration. The functional invariant not only appears in every interaction between the organism and environment, it also:

[Orients] the whole of the successive structures which the mind will then work out in contact with reality. It will thus play the role that [Kant] assigned to the *a priori:* that is to say, [this *functional a priori*] will impose on the structures certain necessary and irreducible conditions. Only the mistake has sometimes been made of regarding the *a priori* as consisting in structures existing ready-made from the beginning of development, whereas if the functional invariant of thought is at work in the most primitive stages, it is only little by little that it impresses itself on consciousness due to the elaboration of structures which are increasingly adapted to the function itself. (Piaget, 1952, p. 3)

In this way, the functioning of "life itself" is formulated as a "progressive equilibrium" (Piaget, 1952, p. 7) worked out through an ordered sequence of stages. But the tendency toward equilibrium is not toward *any* sort of compensation or variation in the organism's structures that will accommodate a new element. Rather, "there is *adaptation* . . . [only] when this variation results in an increase in the interrelationships between the environment and the organism which are favourable to [the organism's] preservation" (Piaget, 1952, p. 5. Emphasis orginal). The modifications that count as adaptive are thus not chaotic or undirected; they are made specifically to create an improved equilibrium in the relation between the organism and the environment.

It is only in light of this teleological sense of equilibrium—equilibrium as an "end" toward which the organism is tending—that the succession of differing structures of organism-environment interactions can be seen as an ordered and comprehensible *sequence.* Moreover, it is only in light of this teleological sense of equilibrium that the succession of structures of organism-environment interactions can be seen to achieve their "perfection" in the concepts and categories and methods of established science. In *The Psychology of Intelligence* (1973, p. 7), Piaget states:

Every structure is to be thought of as a particular form of equilibrium more or less stable within its restricted field and losing its stability on reaching

the limits of the field. But these structures, forming different levels, are to be regarded as succeeding one another according to the law of development, such that each one brings about a more inclusive and stable equilibrium for the processes that emerge from the preceding level.

Development, now understood as a succession of structures oriented toward steadily increasing stability and inclusiveness, "tends towards an all-embracing equilibrium by aiming at the assimilation of the whole of reality" (Piaget, 1973, p. 9).

This tendency toward an all-embracing equilibrium is found in the concepts, categories and methods of established science that, for Piaget, form "an *extension* and *perfection* of all adaptive processes" (Piaget, 1973, p. 7, emphasis original). Again, we see in this Piaget's great participation in an old idea that came to such fruition at the end of the nineteenth and beginning of the twentieth centuries: progress— or better yet, more true to this legacy—that European humanity has developed to the point where it can find its destiny and fulfilment in objective science. We turn now to examine the succession of stages of development that finds its fulfilment in established science.

Stages of Development

Piaget believes that development of knowledge goes through definable stages in a specific sequence. These stages can be characterized as general plateaus of stability or equilibrium. The stages are: sensori-motor knowledge; pre-operational knowledge; concrete operational knowledge; and formal operational knowledge (logico-mathematical knowledge).

The Succession of Stages of Cognitive Development

Sensori-Motor Knowledge

Piaget's first stage of development (0–2 years old), in which children are centered on their immediate physical environment and learn through bodily activities: grabbing, touching, smelling, eating, etc.

The succession of stages of cognitive development in Piaget's genetic epistemology is easy to list, and literally thousands of descriptions of each stage are available: a cursory search on Google gave 9270 hits for "Piaget's stages." Our own brief description of Piaget's **stages of development** follows; we will have a lot more to say about these stages and their characteristics in the next chapter.

Sensori-Motor Knowledge

Sensori-Motor Knowledge is Piaget's first stage of development (0–2 years old), in which children are centered on their immediate physical environment and learn through bodily activities: grabbing, touching, smelling, eating, etc.

The young infant is possessed, initially, only of reflexes that are themselves organized ways of ordering experience—sucking reflexes, grasping ("palmar") reflexes, the reflex whereby the infant's head turns toward an object that touches its cheek, and so on. These are great instinctual adaptive structures that aid the infant's initial survival. Very young children at this stage also have well-developed, if not yet acute, structures of perception; sensory schemata are extremely prevalent. The world is teeming with sensory input—sounds, smells, touches:

> In its beginnings, assimilation is essentially the utilization of the external environment by the subject to nourish his hereditary or acquired schemata. It goes without saying that schemata such as those of sucking, sight, prehension, etc. constantly need to be accommodated to things, and that the necessities of this accommodation often thwart the assimilatory effort. But this accommodation remains so undifferentiated from the assimilatory processes that it does not give rise to any special active behaviour pattern but merely consists in an adjustment of the pattern to the details of the things assimilated. Hence it is natural that at this developmental level the eternal world does not seem formed by permanent objects. In other words, at first the universe consists in mobile and plastic perceptual images centred about personal activity. (Piaget, 1971a, p. 396)

This "state of chaotic undifferentiation" (Piaget, 1971a, p. 397) is an unstable and exclusive form of equilibrium since, by being restricted to the immediate and momentary aspects of the environment, the infant must constantly adapt to each new element which presents itself. These early assimilatory schemata or structures of the infant—inherited and inborn reflexes—are what Piaget calls "global schema[ta]" (1952, p. 35). Simply put, the newborn child tends, for example, to put anything and everything into its mouth and suck on it, having not yet differentiated these schemata into, say, suckable things that provide nourishment and suckable things that provide comfort to the sucking reflex itself.

Even though these very early sensory inputs are

Coordination

A form of accommodation whereby the child integrates two ways of structuring experience, such as "seeing" and "reaching/touching."

Object permanence

The slowly emerging belief, in very young children, that objects continue to exist independently of immediate perceptual experience.

themselves organized by the organism's "assimilatory schemata" (the sense organs), these inputs take time to co-ordinate. **Coordination** is one of the great accommodations that the young child masters to understand, for example, that the object seen and the object grasped are the same object. Grasping, the child realizes, might work in conjunction with seeing. This would be more adaptive and make for a more liveable, more stable world. The young child is thus centred on what is immediate and vivid perceived, through the senses, with all the bodily attachments to those things: touching, smelling, tasting, feeling, grasping, holding, pushing, pulling. This is the sense in which this stage is thus also "motoric"—it is about the slow achievement of motility, movement into the surroundings.

The great Kantian category (for "category," read "form of thinking" or "structure of thinking" or, to use Piaget's term, "schema of thinking") "A = A" has its nebulous beginnings here. Very young children, when presented with objects then covered up or moved, will cease trying to grasp after them, as if the object has ceased to exist. Over the course of the first two years (usually very early on), children slowly develop a sense of what Piaget calls **object permanence**.

This is essentially the belief that "things continue to exist"—A remains A—"even if I don't perceive them immediately." That young girl will go chasing around a tree to find those bubbles that have gone out of sight This is quite an accomplishment, to realize, "The world is not as unstable or fleeting as my immediate perceptual experience." Young children and their parents are engaged in the developmental establishment of this structure of knowledge when playing peekaboo.

Young children are also very imitative, and they begin to enjoy repetitive games, rhymes, songs and stories. Their imaginations begin to flourish. By far the greatest cognitive accomplishment in this first stage of development is the advent of language. The slow development of language (there are libraries writ-

ten on the stages in the development of language) provides a near-miraculous change: the child is no longer restricted to thinking about, invoking, naming, objects that are immediately available. Rather than living in a world of presentation (a world of immediate sensory experiences), the child slowly becomes able to *re-present.* By the tail-end of the sensori-motor stage of development, young children can signify, name and ask for objects that are absent by using a representative of the thing, a "stand in" which they have learned through observation and imitation: a word. They no longer have to stretch their arms towards what they want and express delight. That young girl learns to say "Mummy, I want more bubbles." This indicates another structural change in the child's "method of operation." Children slowly become able to be motivated, not by immediacy and reflex reactions, but by setting goals and attempting to carry them out.

Pre-operational Knowledge

Pre-operational knowledge

Piaget's second stage of development (2–7 years old) in which children become immersed in language and play as forms of knowing.

First, we must note that Piaget does not suggest that the characteristics of the previous stage(s) of development simply disappear once a new stage is entered. Many characteristics central to a certain stage persist or are structurally transformed. In the pre-operational knowledge stage of cognitive development, approximately 2–7 years of age, language takes off, so to speak, and becomes a central engine of the child's exploration of the world. One characteristic from the sensori-motor stage that persists through the pre-operational stage is that the child remains egocentric. This does *not* mean that children at this stage are centred on themselves or selfish. Rather, it means that they have not yet developed a sense of themselves and their own point of view and therefore have difficulty seeing another person's point of view—not because they are centred on their own point of view but because they have not yet grasped the whole idea of *having* a point of view. A young child who announces into the telephone, "It's me," for example, has trouble imagining how

the other person might not know who it is. A great deal of educational energy is focussed on helping children slowly learn that the experiences so immediate to them are not necessarily immediately shared. At this stage, children need to learn to articulate their experience, to share it, speak it, show it and demonstrate it; they are far more able to do so in concrete ways than in abstract or conceptual descriptions.

Coupled with this concrete expression is the dramatic increase in the centrality of play and imagination to development. Young children will spontaneously become involved in what is called "solitary play." A child will move around groups of stuffed animals and talk up a storm, working out elaborate scenarios, rehearsing and repeating things experienced and things imagined—learning all the while about naming, negotiation and narrative structure. Next to coordination, this sort of **consolidation** of assimilatory schemata through repetition is a major form of accommodation and adaptation. In play and through imagination, accommodations can be tested out, troubles can become objects of speculation or trial-and-error, patterns can be established and remembered. Slightly older children become involved in "parallel play," where two or more children will play alongside but essentially independently of each other. Eventually, and (as any teacher of young children knows) sometimes after many instances of troubles arising when two parallel courses of play collide, "co-operative play" emerges, in which the child begins to be able to actually let go of full control over the course of events and play *with* other children, negotiating, co-constructing, and so on. We get a hint here, too, of what is to come. Children become entranced with concretely exploring how things operate, how things work, how they are put together and come apart. Playing with the workings of things becomes endlessly fascinating and time-consuming. Much of this play is deeply sensory and deeply imaginative, full of alluring, powerful images.

This accounts for young children's often intense interest in stories, especially ones that are full of sus-

Consolidation

A form of accommodation whereby the child stabilizes assimilatory schemata through repetition and practice.

pense, adventure, great imaginary figures and monsters, heroes and villains. Children's sense of narrative anticipation and excitement in the face of a rich, imaginative, sensorially laden book full of beautiful pictures and words is uncontainable. In a good children's book, the pictures tell stories at least as compelling as the words. When it comes to learning what the story means, and slowly learning to decode the words themselves, the allure of such images can become an invaluable tool. This makes a case for children coming to understand written language "imaginally," thematically and substantively, rather than simply phonemically. Children learn language narratively, by gathering it into meaningful, belonging-together clusters. A simple example of this is "king, queen, moat, courage, heroes, dragons, castles, battles, horses" and so on. These words are not just stand-ins for lovely, exciting, sensory and bodily things (bold moves, fiery breath, nobility, fear). They are also a cluster of images, ideas and figures that *belong together* in the child's experience of the world. These words form a coherent world. As deeply organizing, assimilatory, constructing beings, children (and adults) crave such coherence and the stability it brings.

By contrast, because young children live imaginatively, a word list that is organized phonemically is rather dull and unalluring: "cat, hat, mat, sat, fat." The phonemic organization "-at words" is very abstract and distant. More bluntly put—and this, I suggest, is a profound and often unnoted consequence of Jean Piaget's insights (Jardine, Clifford & Friesen, 2003a)—understanding and experiencing the phoneme "-at" and the ways in which this phoneme can be prefixed with the letters "c," "h," "m," "s," and "f" is a form of analytic thinking that is a product of a stage of cognitive development to which the young child is not party. As a concept produced by the science of linguistics, "-at" is a logico-mathematically produced assimilatory schema in which the young child has very little concrete interest. This is not to say that children are not interested

in the sounds of language. At this stage (and before it, and after it), the wonderful sounds of language are linked in the life of the child to the giggly, age-old allure of rhymes, poems and nonsense. Young children love to play with words and their sounds, and the dull, decidedly unplayful spelling or writing list "cat, hat, mat, sat" rarely takes advantage of this developmental tendency. Dr. Seuss, on the other hand, does, as does the first-grade child's discovery that my name rhymes with (giggle) "sardine."

There are two final characteristics that point the pre-operational stage towards future developments. First, children in this stage of cognitive development are certainly capable of what is sometimes too loosely called "abstract thinking," but what we mean by that must be fleshed out. After having read image-rich stories about the perilous journeys of various travellers, even very young children can become engaged in profound conversations and speculations about why people go on journeys, why such things are written about, how perils always seem to appear, how such perils can be lessons, and how learning such lessons might be why authors write such things. But this sort of "abstract" thinking—away from the specific, concrete content of any one story—is still what could be neologistically called "concrete abstract thinking." That is to say, children are capable of gathering the images and themes from these stories in substantive ways full of imagery, examples and "body," full of engaged and engaging questions and concerns. If a teacher moves to a new set of stories—about love, affection, obligation and trust, for example—that teacher must recall that previous example, in all its concreteness and particularity, to use it as a model for the new discussions and explorations. The thematizing that children did on journeys in the first instance is not known, experienced or remembered by them as a general and generalizable way of operating. It is known and remembered only in its concreteness, and the teacher will find that that former way of thinking about the various journey-stories must be re-embodied in this

new instance, re-figured. The substance, feel and flow of that former activity must be remembered and re-experienced in order for children to carry it forward into this new territory.

A second characteristic of this pre-operational stage of cognitive development is vital in understanding how it represents a stage on the way to an all-embracing equilibrium. Children near the end of this developmental stage are beginning to be able to explicitly perform very simple operations on objects. Counting, adding, putting things in order, sorting, categorizing, subtracting, are all mathematical "operations" that begin to make sense to children at the end of this stage, thus preparing them for the next.

Concrete Operational Knowledge

Concrete operational knowledge

Piaget's third stage of development (7–11 years old) in which children can know not just about objects in the world but also about operations they perform on an object (adding, subtracting, ordering, etc.), as long as those operations are concrete and visible.

It is no accident that Piaget named the previous stage "pre-operational." Of growing concern to Piaget over the course of the child's cognitive development is how the concepts, categories and methods of established science emerge, and central—one might say *a priori,* universal and necessary—to this emergence are the functional invariants of assimilation, accommodation and their adaptive balance, equilibration. Piaget calls these functional invariants the organism's continuous and invariant "method of operation" in all and every interaction with the environment. What began emerging in the previous stage and now appears dramatically at approximately 7–11 years of age is that the child begins to have a nebulous knowledge not simply of *things in the world* but of his or her own *operations on the world.* In short, their "method of operation" becomes visible to children.

In the stage of concrete operational knowledge children develop the ability to not only have perceptual, empirical knowledge about objects but also to make explicit, very specific operations on such objects—consciously, with knowledge of their own agency. Thus far in development, for the most part, the invariant functions have been operating unconsciously and inexplicitly. Beginning to appear now, albeit in concrete form, is a different type of knowledge. For example, a group of pennies are placed in a circle, and a child counts them. She then starts at a different point on the circle of pennies, counts again and gets the same number. From this sort of example, Piaget extrapolates that what the child is slowly learning is not something about pennies or about some visible, specific starting point on the circle. Rather, the child is slowly learning something about her *actions* and their *organization*. She is learning not about the physical characteristics of the pennies but about the outcomes of the operations she has performed: the operation of counting, enumeration. "Twelve pennies" is neither a physical property of any single penny, nor is it a physical property of the group as a whole. It is, rather, a mathematical "property" that necessarily entails the operation of enumeration, a property tied to the constructive, gathering, synthesizing activity of counting as *an operation* that she *does*.

Take another familiar example: when you place two parallel rows of coins in front of a young child and ask, "Which one has the most?" the child will say that the rows have the same amount. If you then put more space between the pennies to extend one of the rows and ask the same question, very young children will say the longer row has more. This is because, sensorially and motorically, one row is now visibly and undeniably "bigger," and the child is not yet able to detach the knowledge gained from enumeration (in which the number of coins does not change just because you spread them into a longer row) from the perceptually evident fact that one row is now bigger. But in the stage of concrete operational knowledge, children become able to understand that the act of counting the coins and the sensory presentation of the coins are not the same. Moreover—and this is a spectacular breakthrough— the operation of counting is a way of gaining knowledge that is not tethered directly to the objects on which it is performed. Simply put, I can count the chalk, I can count the number of people in the

classroom, I can count the pennies in a circle or in a row. A new sort of knowledge emerges, one that entails getting a reflective grasp on my own ways of operating on the world. I can count things and, moreover, this is a general characteristic of things in the world: things can be counted. This general, operational knowledge—that things are countable, enumerable—is, for Piaget, a different *type* of knowledge than the knowledge that I have three pieces of chalk in my hand.

Piaget maintains, however, that at this early stage of the development of concrete operational knowledge, the knowledge gained is still of necessity *concrete,* still rooted in the sensory and motoric actions of the child. That is to say, for the child, counting is still always counting *something,* a number is still always a number *of things,* and a measure is still always the measure *of something.* This insight has had profound effects on educational theory and practice. It suggests that young children, when first becoming engaged in mathematics, need to act upon and actively manipulate concrete objects—pennies, blocks, sticks—in order for them to effectively understand the operations they are performing. They need to see their operations concretely manifest: a pile of five blocks, remove two of them, how many are left? A pizza with twelve slices, divide them up between the three of us, how many do we each get? And, as teachers know, at first the young child faced with a pile of five blocks from which two have been removed will likely look at the remaining pile and count them out anew, because the child needs to concretely "do" the number that are left in order to concretely understand what it means to have five and take away two.

The idea that young children require the use of concrete objects to manipulate in learning mathematics has become commonplace. And this is also true for most adults—we all require, on occasion, a concrete example, an illustration or a demonstration of an abstract idea we can't quite "picture." Graphs can be understood, but it is best, with very young children, to place concrete representations of the objects on the graph. Organizing the children in a classroom by height does not teach them, for example, how to use the abstract concept of height to organize a group of objects. Rather, going through the concrete process of organizing helps children develop, *out of* that activity, a better and clearer understanding of height measurement as a substantial, image-filled concept. This can be accomplished best if everyone stands up, moves around and sees this series, so that the concreteness of the differences between, say, 44 and 42 and 39 inches tall can be sensorially and concretely grasped. Other classifications of objects can be understood as well, but it is still necessary to make the new experience of "ordering" or "gathering" similarly concrete and active: for example, to sort things by colour by actively picking them out and re-piling them. Therefore, when a classroom of young children are faced with a new task of, say, putting larger to smaller tomatoes from the garden in order of size, it is not useful to ask "Who can tell me what the rules are for doing this task?" As teachers well know, it is much more useful to ask "Who can tell me what we did last week when we organized the . . . ?" This asks the child to "know" the "rule" of ordering by means of their embodied work and in light of a concrete previous example of an activity wherein that rule concretely appeared.

This is a vital point for educators: when we want children of this age to demonstrate their knowledge about how many different sizes of blocks are in a tub, they may need to do more than think about it. Children need to show us what they know, and in order to do that, they may need to redo the knowing by sorting, naming, enumerating and then answering. Moreover, and equally vital, the next day, when asked the same question, they will probably need to do it all over again, because they don't necessarily "hold" this concrete knowledge in their heads as a concept, but rather as concrete organizations of actions (operations) that they can only know about in performing these actions. Only after

repeated experiences like this are children slowly able to abstract from these concrete operational activities and get a glimpse of what forms the core of the next stage of development, formal operational knowledge—knowledge of the abstract organization of the operations themselves, detached fully from any concrete exemplification.

Formal Operational Knowledge

Formal operational knowledge

Piaget's fourth stage of development (11–15+ years old), in which children begin to understand their methods of operation (including logic and math) independently of operating on a concrete object or problem.

At approximately 11–15+ years of age the sort of knowledge requisite of the concepts, categories and methods of established sciences comes into full bloom. Let's go back to the example of knowing that there are three pieces of chalk in my hand. In a commonsense way, in knowing that there are three pieces of chalk in my hand, you do know something about those objects. When we think of what you know according to the previous stage— what you know in a concrete operational way— you know that you counted them and that you could just as well count something else as well; you can detach concretely counting from concretely counting chalk. You can count almost anything. This becomes a charming obsession of some children, who become taken with the numbers of things: How many miles is it to Mars? How many grains of sand are in my hand?

In this new stage of formal operational knowledge, you also are able to gain knowledge simply from a number itself. You can begin to think not just about enumerating physical objects but also about how numbers abstractly work in relation to each other. Numbering, adding, subtracting, multiplying, dividing, measuring, ordering, serializing, graphing—these matters become knowable as orderly, rule-governed, formal, abstract, structured ways of operating. According to Piaget, what a child learns in knowing these ways of operating are the general forms or shapes that knowledge of *any possible object* can take. In coming upon these structured, rule-governed ways of operating on the world, the growing child has come upon a way that knowledge can operate that grows and lives beyond his or her individuality and experience. In knowing concretely that there are three pieces of chalk in my hand, my knowing remains tethered to me and my own experiences; in knowing about numeration in its formal operational sense, I've come upon an instance of "processes common to *all* subjects" (Piaget, 1965a, p. 108, emphasis added). I've come upon a knowledge of the functional or operational character of knowing itself. And, to follow the Kantian logic of knowledge-as-construction, in coming to know the processes or operations common to all subjects, I come to know the general terms in which all subjects can construct the world. To re-cite: "the *a priori* [common to all subjects] conditions of a possible experience in general are at the same time conditions of the possibility of objects of experience" (Kant, 1964, p. 138).

In the stage of formal operations (also called logico-mathematical knowledge) I've discovered, according to Piaget, the logic of objectivity, because I've discovered a knowledge of the invariant functioning or operating of "life itself." This functioning has been going on all along and is common even in the newborn infant, except in that case, the unavoidable processes (the functional invariants of assimilation, accommodation and equilibration) are encumbered by and embodied in structures not yet fully adaptive, not yet fully aware of or in command of those operations. According to Piaget, then, at the logico-mathematical stage of development, I've arrived at a way of knowing that is in command of the functional invariants: the core of the concepts, categories and methods of objective science.

Clearly, "objectivity does not . . . mean independence in relation to the assimilatory activity of intelligence, but simply dissociation from the self and from egocentric subjectivity" (Piaget, 1952, p. 366). Objectivity is not a static relation between the subject and an object but a form of activity that operates in a de-centred manner, away from the exclusive schemata of the individual and toward schemata

Decentration

The process whereby children acquire distance from their immediate experience, knowledge and action and understand that their own point of view may not be shared by others.

common to all individuals (the whole process of **decentration** is itself a fascinating topic in Piaget's work that we won't elaborate on here). Objectivity, far from being an inert state, is a common method of operation, a *methodology*. To know the world in this formal operational way is to "do" science. And, correlatively, established science is most originally and most fundamentally a method of operation.

Even after this long journey, we still haven't directly answered our question: how is it that the concepts, categories and methods of established science form "an extension and perfection of all adaptive processes"? How is it that the concepts, categories and methods of established science provide "an all-embracing equilibrium by aiming at the assimilation of the whole of reality"?

Formal Logic and Mathematics as the Origin of Intelligence

This last twist in Piaget's search for the origins of intelligence is nearly biblical in its import: because of the relationship between logico-mathematical knowledge and the functional invariants that are the origins of intelligence, what comes last is also somehow first. Formal logic and mathematics, which underwrite the methods of operation in established science, are understood by Jean Piaget to embody the functional invariants inherent in "life itself."

Correlative to the developing child slowly decentring away from the individuality and immediacy of concrete experience is a decentring away from the actual situations in which the individual finds him or herself. We become slowly conscious and in explicit command over our invariant and inevitable ways of operating on the world (the functional *a priori*). Thus we also become conscious of and in command over the invariant and inevitable ways that things in the world operate. This, again, is the consequence of constructivism: our ways of operating are a constructing, ordering and organizing demand made upon the world. We are able ahead of time to anticipate "potential" or "virtual" situations (Piaget,

1967, p. 101)—we are able to think about what is possible and what is virtually impossible. Because the assimilatory schemata characteristic of established science are organized around the functional *a priori,* potential or virtual situations can be anticipated, manipulated, controlled and predicted without the organism having to suffer the disequilibrating impact of an actual intrusion of the environment. In other words, we can *think about things:* we can figure them out and, to a degree, affect and control their impact on us by knowing them "objectively," knowing them solely in light of the ways they are constructed vis-à-vis the invariant operations of the organism.

We can therefore deliberately take in hand—but mentally, at a sort of metaphorical arms-length—our immediate well-being and survival, the great functions that define an organism's inevitable and invariant method of operation. We can set forth a hypothesis, an idea or a theory—an assimilatory schema—that we want to check out, and we can explicitly bring to bear upon it events that will attempt to "disequilibrate" it, to "disprove" it. If our original hypothesis becomes shaky, we can accommodate it—differentiate, redefine, consolidate, re-operationalize—and begin again, with the anticipation of either confirming this hypothesis (i.e., reaching some equilibrium) or disconfirming it (i.e., experiencing disequilibrium and the need to accommodate, thus restarting the process). All this can be done formally, logically and objectively. We do not have to physically suffer this process, the way a hungry infant with a functionally similar process of assimilation, accommodation and equilibration suffers. Certainly we can become deeply despondent over a failed experiment. But if we wish to achieve objectivity, we cannot allow this disappointment to enter into the method of operation itself. For a theory to be scientific, then, it has to be kept open to the possibility of being falsified (see Popper, 2002) by future experience. Differently put, for a theory to be scientific, it has to incorporate the possi-

bility of its own disequilibrium and the achievement of a new equilibration, a new theory.

So, to make this final turn, we need to re-cite an extended passage from Piaget's *Origins of Intelligence in Children* (1952, p. 2). The functional *a priori* that defines how life itself operates

> [orients] the whole of the successive structures which the mind will then work out in contact with reality. It will thus play the role that [Kant] assigned to the *a priori:* that is to say, [this functional *a priori*] will impose on the structures certain necessary and irreducible conditions. Only the mistake has sometimes been made of regarding the *a priori* as consisting in structures existing ready-made from the beginning of development, whereas if the functional invariant of thought is at work in the most primitive stages, it is only little by little that it impresses itself on consciousness due to the elaboration of structures which are increasingly adapted to the function itself.

Thus, the sequential development of the structures characteristic of each level of the child's cognitive development is not increasingly better adapted, to the way things somehow "really are" in the world, independently of the functioning of the organism (constructivism has rid us of this naïveté). Rather, over the course of development, we are better and better adapted to *the inevitabilities of adaptation itself.* That is to say, the functions of assimilation, accommodation and equilibration are *a priori,* and the best-adapted structures (most stable and most inclusive) are the ones that are best adapted "to the functioning itself." Development is oriented, therefore, toward continually improving adaptation to the inevitable "organizing activity inherent in life itself" (Piaget, 1952, p. 19).

The peculiarity of the Kantian categories (recall, the Kantian "forms of thinking" that he believed are universal and necessary [*a priori*] to thinking) is that they constitute an extension and perfection of all adaptive processes insofar as they are perfectly adapted to this organizing activity. In this way, the Kantian categories take on the *appearance* of universality and necessity (take on the appearance of being *a priori*) at the end of development because they are perfect expressions of that which *is* universal and necessary: the *functions* of assimilation, accommodation and equilibration (what Piaget calls the functional invariants—the "how" of the functioning —of all interactions between the organism and the environment, *including* logico-mathematical knowledge). Thus "the progress of reason doubtless consists in an increasingly advanced awareness of the organizing activity inherent in life itself" (Piaget, 1952, p. 19). Such an awareness is an "all-embracing assimilatory schema tending to encompassing the whole of reality" since it is an awareness of the organizing activity in terms of which reality itself is constituted.

This helps explain why the sequence of development in Piaget's work moves from sensori-motor knowledge, to pre-operational, to concrete operational, to formal/logical operational knowledge. It has to do with the teleological tendency inherent in adaptation, the sense in which the organism tends toward increasingly stable and inclusive forms of equilibrium. At the highest level of development we have logico-mathematical knowledge, which is in essence a knowledge of the constructive and organizational operations of knowledge itself—knowledge, that is, of the *functioning* that has been going on all along. When we reach the level of formal logic and theoretical mathematics, perfect equilibrium is attained because in these sciences (crystallisations of the methods of established science) we "proceed by the application of perfectly explicit rules, these rules being, of course, the very ones that define the structure under consideration" (Piaget, 1970b, p. 15). That is to say, at the level of logic and mathematics, the rules for doing the operations of logic and mathematics are precisely the rules upon which one operates. Logic and mathematics are thus perfectly equilibrated, for there is no longer any difference between *the operator* (the subject who does logic and mathematics operates only in accord with the rules requisite of logic and mathematics and there-

fore who operates identically to any subject who does logic and mathematics, in accord only with the general and abstract "processes common to all subjects"), *the operations* performed (logical and mathematical operations), and *that which is being operated upon* (an object in the world constructed according to the ordering demands of logic and mathematics).

These three aspects, so different and mixed in previous stages of cognitive development, are now identical. Logic and mathematics thus emerge as a perfect and pure embodiment of the organizing activity inherent in life itself. The equilibrium embodied in logic and mathematics is thus the *telos*, the "end" of development, and paradoxically, also its origin.

We've reached an unusual spot. By reaching this stage of development, we have also reached the origin that has been present all along, the only difference being that now we have attained an explicit *awareness* of that origin. More strongly put, we are no longer buffeted by the constant striving to adapt. We have reached a command over the origin.

Speaking of origins, it would be very naive to believe that Jean Piaget randomly chose the concepts, categories and methods of established science as his object of study and then just happened to find out that they were an extension and perfection of all adaptive processes. Culturally, historically, philosophically, this belief was already widespread in his time—and still is. Most of us still place great stock in those things that objective science tells us, we still believe (in varying degrees) that science is our best hope at knowing the world, to the extent that knowing the world means being able to control, predict and manipulate objects. And, of course, to a certain extent, this is true. The many ways in which objective science has helped us live longer and healthier lives and to have better control over nature and its vagaries are evident. We still trust—or, in some settings, are *required* to trust—the outcomes of an objective experiment more than the narrative stories a teacher might tell of the life of a child.

However, one didn't pursue the sort of search for origins rampant in the late nineteenth and early twentieth centuries without already believing that one's own culture or age would turn out to be "number one." This provides the transition to our next chapter. We must take into consideration the fact that Jean Piaget's descriptions of, interests in and evaluation of the characteristics of each stage of cognitive development were and are only retrospectively chosen. That is to say, it is only in light of the outcome of logic and mathematics that any particular characteristics of how children think about and understand the world are of interest. The good news is that we, as inheritors of his work, are not under such a restriction. Jean Piaget's explorations have opened up a rich territory that goes far beyond the particular interests of genetic epistemology.

GLOSSARY

Accommodation—the functional process whereby the already existing ways of structuring experience that the organism has developed are forced, because of anomalies in the environment, to adjust themselves to new information in order to re-achieve equilibrium between the organism and the environment. Accommodation must always be understood as the accommodation *made by* a structure or schema.

Adaptation—a balance or equilibrium between the organism and the environment. Piaget believes that adaptation goes through stages of development such that each new stage is defined as a more inclusive, more stable equilibrium than the previous stage.

Assimilation—the functional process whereby the organism takes in and structures input from the environment. Assimilation must always be understood as the assimilation of environmental input *to* a structure or schema, an action which is constructive and constitutive of what inputs will be allowed and how they will be organized.

Concrete operational knowledge—a stage of development defined by Piaget as first emerging at around age seven and continuing until approximately age eleven. Its main defining feature is that children are beginning to know not just about objects in the world, but also about the *operations* that they perform on object in the world (adding, subtracting,

ordering, sequencing and so on). At this stage, however, the operations performed are understood only indirectly, only insofar as children are able to concretely manipulate visual objects.

Consolidation—a form of accommodation whereby the child stabilizes his or her assimilatory schemata through repetition and practice.

Coordination—a form of accommodation whereby the child comes to be able to integrate two previously separate ways of structuring experience, such as seeing and reaching/touching, so that the child can see, reach for and grasp an object.

Decentration—the slow process whereby the child is able to distance himself or herself from individual, immediate experience, knowledge and action and comes to understand that one has an individual point of view not necessarily shared by others.

Equilibration/equilibrium—the organism tends toward a stable relationship to the environment, and Piaget suggests that equilibrium is reached in a sequence of stages or plateaus, each new stage being more stable and inclusive than the previous stage. Equilibrium is a balance between accommodation and assimilation.

Formal operational knowledge—a stage of development defined by Piaget as first emerging around age eleven, also known as logico-mathematical knowledge. Its main defining feature is that children are beginning to be able to know about their methods of operating on the world *independently* of operating on some concrete object or problem. The formal operations typical of logic and mathematics fall into this category. At this stage of development, the *a priori,* universal and necessary functional invariants that have been at work all along (assimilation, accommodation and equilibration) become understandable as a deployable and explicit method of operation requisite of established science.

Functional invariants—These are assimilation, accommodation and equilibration, and they define the *a priori* character of *any* relationship between the organism and the environment. Rather than understanding the *a priori* as a set of structures (following Kant), Piaget believes that the *a priori* is functional in character and that the structures described by Kant are those that are best adapted to this invariant, universal and necessary functioning.

Object permanence—the slowly emerging belief that objects are permanent and continue to exist independently of our immediate perceptual experience of them.

Pre-operational knowledge—a stage of knowledge defined by

Piaget as first emerging at around age two and extending until age seven. Its main defining feature is that children are beginning to become fully immersed in language and are highly imaginative and playful. Play, in fact, is their main form of knowing, through active manipulation of objects and persistent questions about how things work, where they have come from and so on.

Sensori-motor knowledge—a stage of development defined by Piaget as the period between birth and two years of age. Its main defining feature is that children are centred on what presents itself immediately and perceptually in their environment. They come to learn and know the world through concrete bodily, motile activities: grabbing things, touching them, smelling them, eating them and so on.

Stages of development—Piaget believes that development of knowledge goes through definable stages in a specific sequence. These stages can be characterized as general plateaus of stability or equilibrium. The stages are: sensori-motor knowledge; pre-operational knowledge; concrete operational knowledge; and formal operational knowledge (logico-mathematical knowledge).

Table of Categories—Kant's Table of Categories parallels his Table of Judgements in structure but lists the ways in which the universal and necessary synthesizing functions of thinking construct and determine how we think about objects in the world (see transcendental logic).

Teleology/teleological—an old idea having to do with something moving toward an end-point (from the Greek *telos* for "end" or "goal"). Piaget understands equilibrium to be a teleological notion. This means that the end point of a stable and inclusive adaptation to the environment (a stable and inclusive stage of development) gives rise to the tendency of the organism towards that end. The functioning of assimilation, accommodation and equilibration, in effect, "drives" the organism toward higher levels of development.

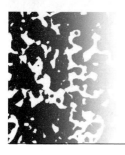

CHAPTER FOUR

Offstage Pedagogical Vignettes

"A Single Truth Alone"

It is difficult to come up with a consistent answer regarding Jean Piaget's views on the real worth of the stages of development. They are certainly worthwhile and necessary to the extent that they led to established science, but it could be argued that they have status for Piaget *only* to that extent. As mentioned at the end of the previous chapter, Piaget's interest in these matters was retrospective. He looked in the stages of development not for the richness and fullness of anything that might appear but only for the developmental precursors of established science.

This leads to an interesting dilemma, especially for those of us who have taken up the Piagetian legacy in educational theory and practice. On one hand, Piaget's careful and dedicated work—his sharp and acute observations of children's lives, his skill at talking with children and following their lead in search of how they were constructing their worlds— allowed us to see that the ways of knowing the world other than those of established science also

have character and integrity. On the other hand, Piaget was interested in the "lower" stages of development *only* insofar as they *fail,* and in such failure, lead to further development and eventually to logic and mathematics.

At his most ungenerous, Piaget tells us that "a single truth alone is acceptable when we are dealing with knowledge in the strictest sense" (1965, pp. 216–17) and that all the ambiguous, multilevel, embodied, imaginative knowing that children and adults engage in is not strictly "knowledge," and that only established science is worthy of that name. Taken thus, it is no surprise when Piaget suggests that children's tales are (albeit developmentally necessary) "deformations" of the truth (1974a, p. 50) and that children often become "duped" "victims of illusion" (1972a, p. 141) when their ways of constructing understanding and meaning become "traps into which [they] consistently fall" (1974a, p. 73). In this light, established science appears to show the true form of things; it appears to be a way to avoid being a trapped dupe of illusion. Because there is a single truth when we are dealing with knowledge in the strict sense, it is little wonder (and yet still a bit of a surprise) that Piaget would say that "the whole perspective of childhood is falsified" (1972a, p. 197). Given his deep developmental interest, such language is understandable, because it is precisely the overcoming of illusion and falsehood by objective science whose eventual developmental emergence is in view.

Piaget is, as we discussed in chapter 1, interested in the genesis of established science, not children and their views. He is interested in what gives rise to such emergence as it appears in the nature of children's ways of constructing the world but only to the extent that it provides a genetic grounding of established science. He does not deeply believe in the indigenous worth of children's constructions, because they prove, in the end, to be not especially adaptive. Children grow up and give up childish ways. Jean Piaget's vision of "a single truth alone" bequeaths us an ambiguous, unsettling legacy.

There is another related dilemma here regarding how Piaget's work can sometimes be taken up by educators, a dilemma for which Piagetian theory gives a good account. Let's recall that compelling passage from David Elkind (1967, xii):

> Once a concept is constructed, it is immediately experienced so that it appears to the subject as a perceptually given property of the object and independent of the subject's own mental activity.

We can equally say that once a teacher (or any person laying out a developmentally organized curriculum guide) understands the stage-specifics of Jean Piaget's theory, it is commonplace for that theory's constructions to become experienced as properties of the object. We can come to transform what was initially a fluidity and multiplicity of insight into rigid, lock-step, unambiguous developmental curriculum sequences that blind us to the fullness and diversity of the children we actually face in the work of teaching and learning.

I suggest that the ways of knowing that Piaget made visible are far more fluid in their appearance and reappearance. They are far more informative for teachers and those who think about curriculum and its guides once they are disconnected from Piaget's own developmental interest. A perhaps unintended insight arose from Piaget's work: beyond the interest of sequencing thinking toward the emergence of established science lies the generous and far more difficult idea of *multiple ways of knowing.* If we let go for a moment of the strictures of developmentalism, we find that there is no "knowledge in the strictest sense," no "single truth" that can usurp the place, power and necessity of other ways of knowing, other truths about the world in its fullness. When a young child precariously tests the limits of balance in a tall stack of blocks, this is a way of coming to know, as is the carpenter's eye for balanced design. And when that carpenter used "3, 4, 5" to understand the measures of wood, that was a way of knowing, as is a mathematician's formal utilization of the Pythagorean Theorem. In the fullness of the human

enterprise, we don't need to choose between these ways of knowing, nor do we need to rank them. We choose between them as the situations we encounter in the world require of us.

We do not, therefore, have to imagine these multiple and diverse ways of knowing as somehow strung along a developmental sequence. Instead, we can imagine them as all belonging to the vast field of human ways. In the classroom, this multiplicity of ways can be brought to bear on a good, rich topic. This might even be how we might define a "good, rich classroom topic": one that can bear a diversity of understanding, of interest, of background and ability. We can imagine the children in our classrooms not as ranked along some line of development or divided up into developmentally organized "groups" but as right there along with us and all the other students, pondering problems and raising questions in their own ways, just as we are there, pondering the same topics in *our* own ways. We, too, as adults, have work to do in order to understand, say, "place-value," in all its complexity in the human inheritance.

When we imagine ways of knowing like *this*, we no longer imagine a classroom *psychologically*, where everyone is locked into their own constructs and where the materials engaged by students are accordingly divvied up into "developmentally appropriate" categories—which always reminds me, following Dressman (1993), of the classroom being like the community of the shopping mall, where we all come together to mind our own (developmentally appropriate) business. Rather, we can imagine the classroom *ecologically*, as a place that sustains difference and whose liveliness and living reality is (inter)dependent upon a play of diverse voices. Imagined ecologically instead of psychologically, the classroom is a place where we all come together to mind the business at hand, each in our own way(s). We can do this only if the topics we are dealing with are *not* developmentally divvied up but rather are presented with a fullness that can sustain the range of possible interests brought to bear on them. We don't have to run ahead, so to speak, of our students to break down the world and its intimate, vital and alluring interconnections into portions doled out in developmentally appropriate practices—we don't have to break those threads of implication and connectedness that make any particular topic meaningful and true.

In light of the wonderful array of ways of knowing that Piaget (and many others) have described, we can do something more ecologically sound in the classroom. Of course, some of the threads of interconnection will trail off beyond a particular child's (or adult's) interest or ability. However, being allowed to experience this "trailing off" gives integrity and a sense of place to the work any one of us will pursue. For example, we can leave in place all the interweavings of the world of "place-value"—its relation to base-ten, to the Roman-numeral system, to the then-controversial introduction of zero into our number system (Seife, 2000), to the ways in which different bases are often utilized, to the ways in which place-value is just like gathering ten popsicle sticks together and putting an elastic band around them and putting that bundle in a new place, and so on—and let our students *find their own ways* in accord with their interests and abilities. By leaving "place-value" where it belongs, in the midst of all its relations, we make it possible for children to see the connections, make the leaps and expand their knowledge and interests beyond our prescriptions of their developmental ability. After all, even first-grade children find the story of how the mathematical community responded when zero was first introduced a rip-roaring tale of intrigue, suspicion and concern. Zero is a very intriguing concept, for children and adults alike, and place-value doesn't work without it. You have to be able to "hold the place open" even if there is nothing in the place, as in the number 20, for example.

By surrounding first-grade children with all the relations to their explorations of place-value, we

protect, strengthen and value their work as part of a common enterprise of the human spirit. Their questions about bundling popsicle sticks are not portioned off as "kids' work" but are understood and visible as the very same work that mathematicians have undergone: a full and legitimate part of coming to know the world. Kids' work is real work. There is no "single truth alone."

Of course, we can certainly provide just a formal definition of place-value and exact rules of how it works and be done with the whole issue. But those rules and exactness still live among all the trailing ways of the world of place and its value. As Ludwig Wittgenstein (1968, p. 36) tells us, we can *draw* boundaries or frontiers in such matters, but we cannot *give* such matters a boundary. Ways of knowing reflect, supplement, enrich, develop and strengthen one another; they cancel out, limit and define differences.

Hence this chapter provides, as the title says, "Offstage Pedagogical Vignettes." These vignettes are explorations of how Jean Piaget's insights can help teachers experience both children's and adults' ways of knowing and their deep *belonging together.*

The Vignettes

Crawling Across the Floor on All Fours

Here is an experiment I often conduct with student-teachers. I say, "You have five seconds to answer this question, and, in attempting to answer it, *you must not move.* Raise your hand once you have the answer: What order do your hands and knees go in when you crawl across the floor on all fours?"

One or two students at most raise their hands in time. Usually all of the students are terribly frustrated when I announce that time is up. They are even more frustrated when I announce, "Okay, the rest of you don't know how to crawl. You failed the test."

This simple example shows something about

sensori-motor knowledge that is vital to a teacher's work. Of course, all of the students know how to crawl. The problem is that they have stored that knowledge not in their heads as an idea or as a mathematically patterned set of abstract operations, but in their bodies. They all know full well that if they had the chance, they could get down on all fours and "do" crawling and then easily and quickly and correctly answer my question. The discussions that follow this exercise are important: how many things do we fully mature adults know in this manner?

Our hands are full of knowledge if we play an instrument. Our bodies are full of knowledge if we play sports or dance, if we know our way around a familiar physical territory, if we know how to handle tools. Our bodies know the proportionality of the Golden Mean that the ancient Greeks first articulated: carpenters and artists can spot it with their eyes and create it with their hands. As writers, we can also understand the "ways of the hand" (Sudnow, 1979) that we have come to learn through repetition and practice: writing is a bodily act, and this act changes when we move from writing in our own hand (Jardine, Graham, Clifford, & Friesen, 2002) to writing with a keyboard, from sitting at a desk to sitting near a stream. We can thus envisage the act of coming to write as an act of disciplining the body as much as the mind.

Taken further, we can also envisage the act of writing as invoking not just the meaning of words but also their physical sonorities: their patterns, their lilt, their music, their beauty.

"Who Can Tell Me What a Triangle Is?"

Student-teachers are often compelled to begin a classroom lesson by getting a sense of what the children already know about a particular topic. This is an old Piagetian commonplace: what are the children bringing to this lesson? Neither children nor adults are empty vessels to be passively filled with the latest lesson but are active, experiencing and experienced agents who will, by their agency, help fashion what

the lesson is about, sometimes in concert with, sometimes in spite of the teacher's best efforts.

One student-teacher decided to find out, as the saying goes, "where the children are at" by starting a first-grade lesson on triangles thus:

"Who can tell me what a triangle is?"

No response.

So the student-teacher proceeded with a lesson based on the assumption that the children didn't know about triangles. The children, of course, became restless and in good teacherly fashion, the teacher understood their restlessness as misbehaviour and began "redirecting" them. This is an all-too-common scenario.

Piaget tells us that young children have an active, sensory and bodily understanding of the world. As with that young girl chasing bubbles, a child's comprehension is deeply *prehensive,* that is, based on physicality, on grasping, on trying to get a literal hold on something. Children's previous knowledge about triangles is therefore probably not stored as an idea whose definition they can produce on demand. Instead it is stored in images and memories; a "triangle" is something they could search out, something they could perhaps draw or locate in a puzzle or painting, something they could handle and whose sides and points they could count. It is "just like a witch's hat" or "pointy," but it isn't necessarily a disembodied idea whose definition they know to articulate as such.

The restlessness that the students experienced in this lesson is a telling epistemological response. When asked for a definition, their bodies engaged but had no outlet. Their restlessness, then, is not misbehaviour but rather a pedagogical clue, courtesy (in part) of the insights of Jean Piaget.

"Sit Still and Pay Attention"

When you are teaching a group of young children and near the back of the class, one child starts swaying back and forth or stands up when you begin to speak, it may be that the child is trying to understand what you are saying by attempting to "do" understanding in a bodily and motoric way. This is why early-childhood-education teachers often "perform" lessons: when opening an orange-juice can, for example, one child is invited to turn the handle on the opener, and the rest are asked to help by stretching their arms up and turning them in the air. This seems at first like childishness, like playful attempts to "trick" children into paying attention. Piaget tells us that it is, on the contrary, a deeply pedagogical, deeply epistemological activity—the act of "doing," knowing-what's-going-on, the act of bodily participating in the construction of paying attention, understanding and knowing. Sometimes a normally restless child is invited to sit beside the teacher and help out during the lesson, not just because it helps redirect the child's attention and contain the restlessness but also because in order to *know,* the child must be allowed to *do.* This is also why there is such uproar in the later years of schooling, when turbulent bodies are stuffed behind small desks and forced to sit still in order to learn.

We now full well how schools, both in their physical layout and in their schedules, are organized around a profound sense of physical containment. We know how hard it can be to contain ourselves when someone drones on and on and won't allow us to speak, to act, to comprehend. We know that as adults, we take notes sometimes, not only in order to be able to recall afterwards what was said in a meeting but in order to pay attention in the first place. Note-taking, a central activity in schools and beyond, is an immediate body function as much as it is idea-, meaning- and memory-driven.

And, finally, we know of the experience when a delicious question arises in the classroom, and hands wiggle frantically and answers get shouted out, breaking the abstract containment of classroom rules—when the students just can't help themselves and a physical burst of energy and excitement results. The whole body of knowledge wants to answer.

Piaget's work helps us see that these phenomena are not just management issues regarding misbe-

haviour but rather are epistemological issues regarding ways of knowing—for children and adults alike.

Speaking of Classroom Management

Parallel to this desired burst of energy runs the student-teacher's worst nightmare. Children who have learned the organization and agreed-upon rules of the classroom tend to embody those rules and organization in the physical presence of the teacher. When the classroom teacher leaves the room, however, she seems to take the rules and organization with her, and the children who seemed to "know" the "rules" a few minutes ago become unruly. The student-teacher must then find ways not just to remind children of the rules in the abstract but to re-embody the rules in his or her own presence in the class. It is important to note this consequence of Piaget's insights: when the children become disrupted by the absence of their familiar teacher, they are not misbehaving. They are, rather, demonstrating that their sense of rule-governedness is not an abstract knowledge of rules but a deeply embodied one, full of investment, trust, presence and anticipation. We can describe a rule as not only a way of anticipating the future but also of feeling secure in the predictability of that future. Treating the children's sudden change when the familiar teacher leaves as misbehaviour misses something about how children of this age construct an understanding of their world.

And before we judge children for behaving better in the presence of the teacher, we should consider how well we drive when there is a police car on our tail. This is not just a matter of "moral reasoning" as both Piaget (1965b) and his follower Lawrence Kohlberg (1989) suggest—i.e., about how we understand "right" and "wrong." It is an epistemological issue about how rules are known and embodied.

Rules, Examples and Recursiveness

Using examples is fundamental to our coming to know the world, and teachers take great and fre-

quent advantage of this phenomenon. Examples are always meant to be examples *of something,* and the movement from the example to an understanding of what it is an example *of* is a complex act.

In a third-grade class, the students were divided up into groups of four. They were given five small squares of paper and asked to divide these up evenly between the members of their groups and to keep track of how they accomplished this. Each way of solving the task was then taken up by the whole class as an example of how to solve the problem.

The first group came up to the blackboard and presented their work. They had dealt out one piece to each of the members of their group and then tore the final piece into four equal pieces and dealt out those. Their work was then represented as 1 + 1/4 for each person.

The second group had placed all five pieces in one pile and tore the whole pile into quarters and then dealt them out. Their work was then represented thus: 1/4 + 1/4 + 1/4 + 1/4 + 1/4 for each person.

The third group divided all five pieces in half, divided up those halves between the four students, and then divided the final two halves in half. Their work was represented as 1/2 + 1/2 + 1/4.

The teacher intervened to ask, "How can all three of these be right?"

Then the fun began—deeply *mathematical* fun at that. The students started to "read" one example in relation to the others: "1 is just four quarters," "1/2 is just two quarters," "If you have five quarters, you can put four of them together and get 1 and you've got one quarter left, just like the first group's solution," and so on.

What is exciting here is that each new answer was not understood as just one more example to be added to the list. Each example made all the previous examples more interesting, more complex, more reasonable and sensible than they might have been on their own. Thus the conversation began to act recursively. That is to say, instead of a simple additive sequence of examples, each example began to

enrich the others and changed how they appeared and how they could be understood. Before conversation broke out, this activity was little more than show-and-tell blessed with the faint praise: "That's a really interesting way to do it. Let's see what the next group did." But after conversation broke out, each group's work was strengthened by the presence of the others. The next group's answer was experienced as more than just "their answer." Their answer was experienced as also *about "my answer."* A student listens to the answers of other students not just to find out what they did but to find out something about his or her own work—to learn something from outside the boundaries of his or her own constructs. In this vignette, the answers were taken up and explored as something more than individual psychological constructs. Through the conversation that ensued, the answers slowly began to *belong together* in a co-constructed body of mathematical knowledge in which every answer had an important place. In this new, growing body of mathematical knowledge, any individual's or group's work becomes irreplaceable, because the whole body of work would have been different without it. Each answer is recursive, folding back into the way in which the whole is constituted and understood, back into the way in which any part of that whole is articulated.

In this way, the work of understanding examples as examples of a slowly emerging "something" is produced substantially, in image-laden ways, full of concrete instances and illustrations. The work of understanding fractions in our story was not accomplished through providing abstract rules and then looking for examples but by providing examples and, from that, cultivating an embodied and emergent sense of the rules that grow out of the examples, out of the concrete conversations and questions. Again, hints of Jean Piaget's legacy.

"Blueberries for Sal"

Curriculum requirements are often listed as isolated and developmentally sequenced concepts and skills that children must come to master in a particular grade. Moreover, they are often described in ways that encourage, or at least allow, the teacher to teach these matters in isolated ways. This isolation can certainly help clarify various aspects of a particular discipline, but it is all too easy to forget that in fact, these aspects do not live in isolation. However, the discrete way in which developmentalism often outlines these matters can have a profound effect on how we imagine teaching and learning to occur. We can come to teach isolated lessons, with all the formality and lack of imagination that the curriculum guide specifies, because we too easily believe that the matters it details *are* in fact isolated.

One of the gifts of Piaget's work is that it helps us recognize that this sense of isolation—whereby we can control, predict and manipulate classroom events as if they were objective states of affairs by breaking down lesson topics into their component parts—is produced by the ways of knowing codified in established science. Logico-mathematically driven analysis, by its very nature, breaks apart the very things that children (and, I suggest, adult nonscientists) hold together. It breaks apart the deep narrative patterns of embodied knowing in the name of a scientific analysis of child development and its stages. It performs a parallel breakdown of the great living disciplines of writing, reading and mathematics and so on. It then becomes the work of the teacher to find ways to put back into place that which has been thus analysed and isolated. Following is an example.

In an early-childhood-education curriculum-methods class, an older student-teacher, with over a decade of experience teaching very young children in a nonschool setting, brought into our curriculum class one of her favourite books, *Blueberries for Sal* by Robert McClosky (1976). This had been a personal favourite from her own childhood, for her own children and in her work with children, and she was invited to read it to the class.

Her own pleasure over this book was obvious. It tells the tale of a woman and her young daughter out

picking blueberries on a hillside, and how they meet up with a mother bear and her cub doing precisely the same things, and how the "young cubs" in both cases eat juicy handfuls and how they end up following the wrong mother. When she finished, another student asked her how she was going to "use it" in her practicum class (a typical formulation of many student-teachers, and in its own way, quite telling—our mutual pleasure needed to lead to practical application, a sense of what to do next).

She said, "I think I can probably use this book to teach prediction."

"Prediction" was listed in the Alberta Language Arts Curriculum Guide as a skill that young children should cultivate. From what had already gone on in the story, the children could learn to predict what might come next. Very often, this is achieved in a rather artificial, stilted manner: children are asked to predict what comes next, the teacher reads on in the book, and children learn about the status of their predictions. This requires, however, an often unpleasant sense of interruption and articulation. Right in the middle of being carried along with the movement of a story, we halt things, because we are required as teachers to help children articulate what they are in fact *living* in the movement of the story. Right at the moment when we want to go on, we stop and talk about wanting to go on, and we are made the agents and articulators of prediction right at the moment when our own agency was in suspense, carried along by the agency of the book and *its* movement.

"I'm not sure that that is what that book is really about." This comment by a third student in the class sounded harsh at first. But as we proceeded to address the book, the first student's love of it, and its "use" in the classroom, we had a wonderful conversation about what might be really going on in the book: its allures, its tales, its teachings.

The use of this book for teaching prediction would not be altogether incorrect. It is clearly a surface feature of the text that the pages are deliberately set up to entice involvement, anticipation and participation with the funny pleasures of seeing the wrong children with the wrong mothers. But there are also more complex things at work. Over the course of a three-hour class, we talked about how the very presence of that human mother and child gathering blueberries offers a more subtle, earthy lesson in prediction: we can read the signs of what is coming (winter), its terrible "predictability," and the need to gather food in preparation for that eventuality. The mother bear and her cub participated, in their own way, in this same knowledge of what was to come. The humans prepared by gathering and preserving what can be eaten later in the winter; the bears prepared by eating and preserving in their own bodies the ability to survive during hibernation. Ravens and their kin are also in the story, anticipating in their own ways what is to come.

And, too, the young human girl is, as Piaget's work suggests, taken with the concrete and sensuous immediacy of the task. She is constantly putting her hand into her mother's pail of berries and eating (just like the bear cub will do when it starts following the human mother). She sits beside a bush, picking and eating her fill. The sense of preserving for the future that the mother knows is something her child must still come to learn, and we can be assured that the mother, too, ate her fill while also collecting for the future.

In our class, we also thought through this place where these families of relations had met, this hill and its bounty that can sustain similarities and differences in anticipation, this lovely ecological sense that these children and their mothers, these coming seasons and seasonality somehow belong together in the embrace of a place that sustains them all, each in their own way.

It began to appear that "prediction" is not simply a language-arts ability to anticipate or guess or giggle over what the next page of a book might hold. This, of course, is not to deny that there are great pleasures to be had in belly-laughing with young children over such textual anticipations, or

dwelling, with some books, in the fear of what might be coming. It is only to say that the isolated language-arts curriculum specification of prediction is not so isolated after all, that it belongs in a rich array of relations and kin.

The student-teacher who originally brought in the book reported, weeks later, that the children had constructed their own version of the hill and made human, bear and raven figures for it. They had talked about the environment of the place and what it needed in order to sustain this variety of creatures. They had ended up studying hibernation and what we, too, need to prepare ourselves for the cold and darkness to come.

And as they listened to her reading the book, the children knew full well that on the next page, after the bear-cub had mistakenly started following the human mother, sure enough, the girl-child would end up following the mother bear. The curriculum got "covered," not by being taught as an isolated skill but by being surrounded with all its relations.

By the Way

That same student-teacher helped us learn another lesson. She was placed in a third-grade class and was worried over the fact that most of the children did not know how to read.

"I've decided that I need to go back to the beginning," she said. "What I'm going to do is place individual words on some flash cards organized around specific letters and sounds and have the children start practicing these, memorizing them and writing them out in their journals. We'll sound some of them out each day and slowly build a list."

With all her years of experience with young children, it was astonishing that she had fallen prey so easily to the belief that the *products* of an analytic breakdown of language somehow constituted "the beginning."

"That's not the beginning," I said. "You know this. Tell me, how do children *actually* begin learning about stories, about how to read and write?"

"Well, they crawl up into your lap with their favourite book and ask you to read it, sometimes over and over again."

This way of coming to know language, both written and oral—that the words "bear," "raven," "girl," "mother," "blueberries" and "hill" *belong together*—is a much more meaningful enticement to writing and to learning to write. So this student-teacher built a list of "words on the hill" that belonged together on that hill and in the stories it held.

Because of Piaget's generous unfolding of the ways of children (and of adults), we can now experience a terrible pedagogical shock. The meaningless rows of phonemically organized "spelling words" with which these children had been surrounded in their classroom were (at least in part) *causing* the children's "inability" to write because the rows deliberately cut the threads that knit together the children's ways of knowing the world. Breaking words apart into their sounds can easily break apart the ways in which language itself is meaningfully held together. The importation of logico-mathematically divided and subdivided analyses of "the basics" (Jardine, Clifford & Friesen, 2003a) of language back into the indigenous ways of childhood actually falsifies under-standing, actually undermines the child's (and the adult's) ability to learn the ways of the world.

On "Family Resemblance"

A great deal of our understanding of the world is deeply analogical and metaphorical in nature. We often reason and speak in terms of what Ludwig Wittgenstein (1968, p. 32) called "family resem-blances," through which one thing is experienced as resembling the other, as being in the same family or being the same "kind" of thing; we know about something because "this is like that." Instead of strictly adhering to a notion of identity essential to logic and mathematics (where A either *is* or *is not* the same as B), a great deal of our everyday thinking works differently. This thinking-by-resemblance is a

rich and substantial and pervasive way in which we know the world.

Piaget has noted (1965a, p. 6), following from a remark by Henri Bergson, how there has been a shift in the sciences from an interest in kinds (which fit together via resemblance, similarity, analogy and the like) to an interest in laws (which require a fitting together by identity—the extent to which two things follow a law is the extent to which they are identical). This interest in kinds is easily seen in the great taxonomies of Linnaeus; his work on kingdoms, genera, species, subspecies and families and kinship-relations and other relations of kind is still taught in supplemented and modified forms (see Jardine in press). The shift to laws is evident in how current DNA testing relies not on resemblance but on mathematizable laws of identity. Even though a scientist must at some point make a judgement as to the resemblance between two pieces of DNA evidence, that resemblance must fall under the laws governing statistics: we are 98.8% sure that these two DNA samples are identical, we don't just "see" a resemblance.

This phenomenon of a knowledge of kinds points to a lovely way of knowing commonplace in children and adults alike (in which children and adults are "of a kind," one might say): *collecting* kinds of things (see Shepard, 1996). This way of knowing the world can be understood, quite literally, as gathering something. Insects, hockey cards, Duke Ellington CDs, *National Geographic* magazines, even small rocks gathered from places you've visited: these gatherings are relations of kind, not relations of law. They are relations of family resemblance, not relations of identity. Note that the lists we produced in chapter 3 (king, queen, castle, moat, dragon) and in this chapter (mothers, daughters, bears, humans, ravens; preserving, anticipating, seasonality, hibernation, preparation) belong together by resemblance, or by analogy. These are *gatherings* of words.

Logico-mathematical thinking will demand of

such analogies that they can be parsed into lists of "same" and "different." This is a common activity in schools: How are the bear and its cub *the same* as the human mother and daughter? How are they *different?* The case has been made that parsing of family resemblances into sameness and difference in fact does not account fully for this way of knowing the world. Consider Ludwig Wittgenstein's description of "family resemblance":

> As in spinning a thread, we twist fibre on fibre. And the strength of the thread does not reside in the fact that some one fibre runs through its whole length, but in the overlapping of many fibres. Don't say "There *must* be something common" . . . but *look and see* whether there is anything common to all. For if you look at them you will not see something that is common to *all*, but similarities, relationships, and a whole series of them at that. To repeat: don't think but look! We see a complicated network of similarities, overlapping and criss-crossing: sometimes overall similarities, sometimes similarities of detail. I can think of no better expression to characterize these similarities than "family resemblances" [*Familienahnlichkeiten*]. (Wittgenstein 1968, p. 32)

Analogical thinking

Thinking by resemblance, according to kind and similarity, rather than law and identity.

Great arguments regarding the nature of **analogical thinking**—thinking by resemblance, according to kind, similarity, rather than identity and difference—are longstanding in the history of European philosophical thought. Piaget's work has given us a glimpse of how the reliance of logico-mathematical knowledge on identity and difference just might distort our understanding of analogical thinking that works in terms of family resemblance.

Analogical thinking involves the development and exploration of likenesses, similarities, correspondences and parallels between ways of knowing, clusters of images and worlds of discourse: the etymological root of "analogy" is parallel [*ana*] and sense [*logos*]. Such parallels resist the collapse of one thing into another (that is, into shared "identity"), while also resisting the isolation of such realms (into "difference"). Analogies involve the dialogue *between* such realms, a dialogue that sustains a "sim-

ilarity-in-difference" (Norris-Clarke, 1976, p. 66). Recall the students' solutions to dividing up the five slips of paper between four people. Their solutions were not the same, but neither were they simply different. Understanding and exploring an analogy or family resemblance, therefore, is not a matter of discovering some discursive univocal term that makes both sides of the analogy the same or collapses Wittgenstein's "network of similarities, overlapping and criss-crossing" into literal terms applicable to both sides of the analogy. Rather, understanding analogies involves the exploration of the tension that is sustained between similarity and difference, a tension that cannot, in principle, be discursively cashed out in just so many words (Jardine & Morgan, 1987). Understanding an analogy is a matter of becoming party to the conversation between differing realms of discourse that the analogy opens up, of "getting in on" the conversation.

The compelling and powerful character of analogies is not found in *solving* such kinships, as if they were "problems" that could find their resolution in translation into literal, univocal discourse. They are not "accidents" that need to be "fixed," or mere decorative marginalia to the true text of language. Rather, they gain their power precisely in their *resistance* to being "solved." It is because of this resistance to being solved that potent analogies can always be readdressed and remain vivid in our imagination and ways of knowing the world. The family resemblance explored in reading *Blueberries for Sal* might just re-emerge years later in a seventh-grade exploration of animals and their habitats or in a social-studies exploration of the diversities of cultures and their ways. The conversation that a family resemblance opens up can always be taken up anew. In that conversation about *Blueberries for Sal,* we may determine that both "sides" of the analogy—the human mother/child and the bear mother/child—involve, say, "care and attention." We find, however, in exploring this idea of "care and attention" that far from being a way in which these two families are *iden-*

tical, "care and attention" are themselves understood analogously. These two families are alike in care and attention, but again, neither simply identical nor different. This way of knowing thus resists developing into and being thus developmentally replaced by the sort of knowing requisite of established science.

Norris-Clarke points out another feature of the analogical language that rings true to Jean Piaget's descriptions of the ways of knowing of young children. Understanding a family resemblance requires "running up and down the known *range* of cases to which it applies, by actually calling up the spectrum of *different* exemplifications, and then *catching the point*" (1976, p. 67, emphasis original). This is a telling point. To deeply and fully understand an analogical term, we must cover a range of its exemplifications and catch the point of the analogy that cannot be said abstractly and independently in so many words. This is not a matter of refusal to be specific. Rather, it is something that teachers of young children understand as a matter of course: the meaning of the things that have been gathered together in the conversation about *Blueberries for Sal* is embodied and known *in and through* its diverse instantiations. The family resemblance *is* (analogically speaking) its diverse instances. It is not hovering "above" them (another lovely analogical term) as an abstract, disembodied concept. Thus, "there is quite a bit of 'give,' 'flexibility,' indeterminacy or vagueness right within the concept itself, with the result that the meaning remains essentially incomplete, so underdetermined that it cannot be clearly understood until further reference is made to some mode or modes of realization" (Norris-Clarke, 1976, p. 67). To understand an analogical term, to grasp the import of a family resemblance, is not a matter of pursuing the sort of "condensing [and] unifying" (Hillman, 1983, p. 51) requisite of logical and mathematical knowing. We must allow it, rather, "to expand to its full analogous breadth of illuminative meaning" (Norris-Clarke, 1976, p. 72). Only in such breadth does the family resemblance emerge in its fullness

and depth of meaning. Moreover, "whenever [such an analogical term] tries to become too precise, it contracts to become identical with just one of its modes and loses its analogical function" (Norris-Clarke, 1976, pp. 69–70). In such a loss, the world is narrowed.

Mathematical Family Resemblances

In educational theory and practice, an acceptance and understanding of the ways of knowing described by family resemblance, analogy, allegory, metaphor and story are commonplace in, for example, language arts and social studies. This family-resemblance way of knowing and understanding is common, for example, not only in the composition of literature but in our attraction to it: people going through the *kinds* of things we recognize in our own lives, facing the same *kinds* of dilemmas or joys or sorrows. Thinking and understanding according to resemblance is also common in our everyday talk with each other, children and adults alike. We ask first graders to imagine what it was like for a character in a book about the Middle Ages to live without electricity: What would that be *like* in the winter for a wolf? Why would an author say that the villain is *like* a wolf? Or that a melody is *like* a soft summer breeze? In these disciplines of language arts and social studies (the "softer" disciplines, one might say, evoking yet another meaningful way of knowing how language arts and social studies belong together differently than, say, mathematics and the other "hard" sciences) analogical, allegorical, metaphorical, image-laden language is not simply a stage on the way to the formalities of objective language. It is another way of knowing, rife, of course, with ambiguity, intrigue and the necessary possibility of misunderstanding. That is its power.

However—and this again is a breakthrough owed to Piaget's profound insights into the ways of knowing of young children—these ways of knowing are also commonplace *in mathematical thinking itself.*

In one of my curriculum-methods classes, I asked

my students the following question: "In exactly what sense is 198 a *bigger* number than 55?"

This question initially caused quite a bit of confusion and frustration, because there isn't *exactly* a sense in which the term "bigger" is used in this case. However, all of us knew that this is a normal, sensible and meaningful way to talk. We implicitly and easily draw an analogy between physical size and numerical quantity. Consider how a young child stretches out her arms when she talks about a picture of "millions of butterflies" covering South American trees. Consider how Carl Sagan used to say "billions of stars," stretching out the word, exaggerating the tone as if to invoke a resemblance between the enormity of the number and the enormity of the expression of it (see Jardine, 1994; 1998).

Recall, too, how we also unproblematically talk about 198 being a *higher* number than 55. This interweaves in our imagination with a child building a higher and higher stack of blocks, with the fact that we can meaningfully speak of "counting *up* to ten," or with the fact that growing older (a numerically "higher" age) means growing up. So, is it too much to say that the progression of higher and higher numbers orients to infinity (to God, the most high)? Or that numbers that fall, so to speak, below the ground (below the starting point, below where we stand, below "(ground) zero" have a dark and negative character? Or is it too much to say that when counting "higher and higher" quantities, we must, by analogy, keep track of them by consistently bringing them back to earth, back to base, the way that we use "base ten" as a way of preventing the pile from spiralling upwards? These are ways of keeping the number at our fingertips, and we therefore organize numbers into groups we can manage or handle, into "handfuls." Perhaps the analogical idea of "place-value" belongs here, too—*where* we place something has an effect on its value (a 2 in the "tens place" is not the same as a 2 in the "hundreds place"). Perhaps the ways in which the periodic table in chemistry is itself organized around place-value (where the row

or column in which an element has a place is itself informative as to the kind of element it is) does as well.

Student-teachers are consistently amazed at what sort of knowledge they "stumble" on when they realize that we commonly use base ten, and that numbers are sometimes called "digits," and we have ten fingers (also called "digits"). These same student-teachers are constantly faced with parents who worry that their child counts on their fingers, just like I do when I want to emphasize a list of things for student-teachers to remember: "First of all," (my hands go up in front of me, one index finger indicating "point number one") "secondly," (I raise two fingers), and so on, the number of points I wish to emphasize being equal to the number of fingers.

Another analogy of this way of thinking: several years ago, a seven-year-old friend of my son came to visit, and I told him about the huge pond in our neighbour's field. The spring runoff had created a slough about eight feet deep. After discussing that it would be over his head if he fell in, over my son's head, and even over *my* head, he asked, "If a hundred-year-old man stepped in it, would it be over *his* head, too?"

I answered, "Yes, it's *that* deep."

This response is, I suggest, deeply Piagetian. But when I told this tale to a mathematics-curriculum colleague at the University of Calgary, I received the comment, "Isn't it cute when children get things mixed up?"

This is the point at which this idea of family resemblance really hits home in relation to Piaget's work. Our "adult" ways of thinking about the world are not different than those of children, and neither are they simply the same. They are *alike*. Differently put, children's and adult's ways of knowing are "of a kind." Differently put again, children are our kin. Our ways of knowing *belong together* in relationship of *kind*, of *kinship*.

Surprisingly enough, such thinking is profoundly commonplace in the thinking of "established sci-

ence." Although established science may in the end require a logico-mathematical account of its knowing, it often has its *actual* origin in the deep experience of resemblance. Consider, from James Watson's *The Double Helix: A Personal Account of the Discovery of the Structure of DNA:*

> Back in my rooms I lit the coal fire, knowing there was no chance that the sight of my breath would disappear before I was ready for bed. With my fingers too cold to write legibly I huddled next to the fireplace, daydreaming about how several DNA chains could fold together in a pretty and hopefully scientific manner. (Watson n.d.)

"Pretty and hopefully scientific": a great analogical imagining of wheeling, interweaving helixes in a fireplace, precisely the sort of imagining that is *not* talked about within the boundaries of the method of operation of established science (more on this point in the next chapter).

Even when we hear Piaget speak about "*stages* of development," we imagine something *like* platforms, something *akin to* visually pictureable "levels" ascending in stepwise fashion. We spontaneously "picture" Piaget's stages of development as proceeding *upwards,* just like "growing up," which is itself an analogue for the movement from the body (sensorimotor knowledge) to the mind (logico-mathematical knowledge): growing up is "climbing up into our heads," as Ursula Le Guin called it (1987, p. 11).

"It's Not Nonliving, It's Dead"

In one of his earlier works, *The Child's Conception of the World* (1974a, originally published in 1926, Piaget conducted a wonderful series of conversations with young children regarding their images of how things come about in the world, where they come from and how they are *caused*. His central interest, of course, was in how the idea of mechanical causality, requisite of established science, slowly arises in the thinking of children, but what he came upon in the meantime is fascinating: artificialism and animism.

Artificialism

The belief that things are artefacts created or caused or constructed by someone.

Animism

The belief that anything that moves is alive.

Artificialism is not a belief that things are artificial, but that they are artefacts. Artificialism can be described thus: because of the child's intimate knowledge of the doings of his immediate world, because of his intimate knowledge, too, of the doings of his elders, one way of accounting for things is to say that anything that exists was caused or created or constructed or made *by someone*. Who made the clouds? Who created worms? Who makes the sun shine? These are common pre-operational speculations, but they are not just that. Years ago, when I was having an all-too-typical teenaged argument with my mother about religion, she said, "Well, if God didn't make Jupiter, then who did? Answer me that." An object cannot exist unless it was produced by "someone."

Animism is a fascinating way of making sense of the world: anything that moves, that is "animate," is *alive*. In a first-grade class I visited recently as university practicum supervisor, the children were learning the science curriculum requirement regarding the differences between "living" and "nonliving." When I arrived, the student-teachers handed me an 8 ½ x 11 sheet of paper divided in half with a black line, with the words "living" and "nonliving" at the top of each column. The children were then divided up between eight adults, myself included, and, after a brief discussion, we were sent out onto the playground to search for objects and decide where they might be placed on the chart we were given.

Of course, the children took advantage of the "university guy," asking me if they could search by the playground equipment. "Sure," I said—and then promptly got a reminder of how children know and understand and live in the world. But once I got them all off the play equipment and "redirected" to the task at hand, our group quickly checked out cars and dogs walking by. One child then picked up a popsicle stick.

"Nonliving," one child insisted.

Another said, "That's not nonliving. It's dead. That's different."

"Write that down," I insisted. "Here, I'll help."

The children had been encouraged as well to simply make drawings on the paper if they had trouble with the writing, to do whatever might help remind them when we gathered to talk later in the classroom. To know about the decisions you made and to remember them does not necessarily require words; images will do. Thus, the children were allowed precisely the same allowance we need as adults. No one wanted this to turn into a lesson on an individual child's ability to write. That in itself was recognition of multiple ways of knowing.

Later, all of us gathered together and the student-teachers, on a large version of our worksheets, started taking down children's discoveries, probing for why they chose to put things where they did, encouraging them to "make a case" for their thinking and decisions. Again, there was a deep recognition that how children think is as interesting and pedagogically important as the particular conclusions at which they arrive.

I nudged a child in my group.

"We couldn't decide where to put a popsicle stick," the child said. "She said it's 'nonliving,' and I think it's dead."

"They were in *your* group, right?" the student-teacher said, smiling at me, and we had a good laugh with the kids about "university teachers" and the odd questions they can bring. Great debates and arguments about the differences between "nonliving" and "dead" ensued.

Then one child said, "I don't know where to put the sun." This time, a *huge* debate broke out, with questions and counterquestions, examples and counterexamples. The intellectual level of this debate was astonishing.

"It keeps us alive so it *has* to be alive."

"It's just a big fire."

"It moves through the sky every day."

A similar conversation took place between Jean Piaget and an eight-year-old child: "'Does the sun know anything?' 'Yes, it heats.' 'Does the moon

know it shines?' 'Yes.' 'Why?' 'Because it shows us the way at night'" (Piaget, 1974a, pp. 205–6).

In our own classroom, for the moment, "the sun" was printed on the line between "living" and "nonliving." What was most compelling about this vigorous conversation was that these children were recapitulating ancient debates, and their troubles were not simply the product of being too young to know better. Teachers surround and immerse children in stories (written by adults) that are full of animate objects, full of the still-powerful belief that the world is *alive* far beyond the reaches of mechanical causality, that it has ways and agencies. We live in a world where ideas can have agency and effect and power. We all know how our ancestors have variously named the sun a god in recognition of its power, and we recognize a sense of deep dependence and frailty in the face of its gifts. Great scientists propose that the earth as a whole is itself a living being, named after a goddess, Gaia. Saint Francis called the sun his brother, and such calling was not simply foolishness, nor does established science straightforwardly and obviously "know better," nor is one way of knowing where the sun belongs somehow destined to replace the other (see Jardine, 2003).

Allowing this conversation "to expand to its full analogous breadth of illuminative meaning" (Norris-Clarke, 1976, p. 72) called up some great and difficult truths that go beyond any "knowledge in the strictest sense." First-grade conversations about the sun—in this classroom and many others—are not new, trivial or easy, and neither are they yet decided once and for all time. What was wonderful in this instance was that the specific and particular line between living and nonliving as prescribed in the science curriculum guide became visible to the adults and children in this class as an age-old *decision* that was made as to how things are to be understood. Allowing ourselves to explore the controversy over where to put the sun made visible how deliberate and specific the ways are in which established science makes such divisions—and how this division

has been and can be reasonably made otherwise, if we give up on the idea of "a single truth." The particular ways of knowing indigenous to established science were thus able to be put into a much richer context of possibilities of knowing.

Giving up on the idea of a single truth doesn't mean teachers have to give way to a sort of Romantic critique of the seeming coldness and objectivity of established science in favour of literature, poetry, emotion, stories and the like. On the contrary, by allowing these different ways of knowing to each have a life of their own, *each of them* becomes exquisite and irreplaceable. Established science (which, of course, underwrites the science curriculum guide's criteria for the distinction between living and nonliving) becomes visible as *a* way of knowing, not just *the* way of knowing. We learn to embrace, understand and pursue it in a full awareness of its limitedness and particularity and difference.

Or, as Jean Piaget (1952, p. 19, emphasis added) put it:

> From its beginnings, due to the hereditary adaptations of the organism, intelligence finds itself entangled in a network of relations between the organism and the environment. Intelligence does not therefore appear as a power of reflection independent of the particular position which the organism occupies in the university, but is linked, from the very outset, by biological apriorities. It is not at all an independent absolute, but is a relationship *among others* between organism and environment.

Only when the children in this class were allowed to understand the scientific way of knowing the difference between living and nonliving as one way of knowing these matters *among others* were they able to ask questions about the proper place of the ways of knowing specific to established science. Teaching the ways of knowing of established science in isolation from all their relations and kin—taught as it is more often than not, as the "single truth alone" about matters of living and nonliving—in fact falsely portrays established science. It suggests science does not live among the great arrays of human ways of

knowing, as if it does not have an important, sometimes contested, sometimes essential place amid such ways.

Again, despite Piaget's call for "a single truth alone," his own work, paradoxically, can give us a way to sidestep this image of singularity. He can help us articulate the *belonging together* of ways of knowing in the human enterprise of understanding the world.

Dolly the Sheep

A group of seventh-grade students in a class taught by Pat Clifford and Sharon Friesen (see Clifford & Friesen, 2003) were given a wide berth to explore the (mandated Alberta Science Curriculum) question of "natural and manufactured structures." The classroom assignment was, basically, choose a natural and a manufactured structure and explore them, their similarities, differences, designs, purposes, aesthetics, shapes, strengths, character, conflicts.

When I stumbled into this classroom one morning, Pat warned me that one student, Richard, wanted to talk with me as soon as possible. With Sharon and Pat's encouragement, Richard had come to trust me to take his philosophical ventures seriously. What occurred turned out to be one of those wonderful moments that sometimes happen in classrooms, a moment in which a student comes to know, consciously or not, that the question he or she has is for you and no one else.

Richard was, as Pat put it, sometimes a bit like a cat with a chewed-up mole who sneaks into the house, plops it on your shoe and casually sashays away, grinning as only cats can.

"I want to do Dolly the sheep for my 'structures' project," he announced. "But I can't figure it out. Is she a natural structure, or a manufactured one?"

Suddenly, unexpectedly, beyond the watchful monitor of schooling, a curriculum-guide distinction that was supposed to be a "given"—the well-defined difference between "natural" and "manufactured" structures—was no longer a given. Richard's question about Dolly the sheep at first seemed to be working against the clear, rule-governed curriculum guidelines. However, what appeared to be against the rules turned out to be also *on behalf of the rules.*

Natural and manufactured structures or the seeming pigeonholes that required students to just choose examples to fit the predefined categories turned out to be nothing of the kind. Richard's choice of Dolly the sheep demonstrated that the distinction between "natural" and "manufactured" was not settled but open to question. And here's the real humiliation as we ponder his choice and its ramifications: we get a fleeting glimpse that that distinction, even as it forms part of established science, *has never been a "given."* It is, *in its very nature as a scientific phenomenon,* always and necessarily open to the future, open to further debate, further experience, further "accommodation" to future events. It has always been open, in spite of confident curriculum-guide pronouncements or the feigned confidences of provincial or state testing (see Jardine, in press).

With Richard's question, a closed curriculum requirement suddenly was called into question, and by being called into question, it became visible as a *scientific* quandary. Here is another schooled phenomenon that Jean Piaget's work makes visible for us: those fake and feigned, profoundly nonscientific "experiments" that form a great part of "science curriculum"—experiments whose outcomes are already understood by teachers and students alike—are not really science at all.

Pythagorean Shadows

A few years ago, on a bitterly cold Alberta winter day like, near enough to winter solstice that the sun was very low, I was out on an elementary school playground with a twelve-year-old boy. We had just been inside in a classroom of around sixty students, quarrelling in interesting, heated ways about dropping perpendiculars and bisecting angles with only compasses, pencils and straight-edges in hand (see

Jardine, Clifford & Friesen, 2003a), invoking the ghost of Pythagoras, his secret cult and his great geometrical insights. Out on the playground, the boy was facing south, his toes touching the tip of a pine tree's shadow.

I can only vaguely recount what the boy said. He talked about having been on that playground in the summer, when the shadows had been so short because of how high the sun was, and now, he noticed, the shadows were so long and the sun was so low. He was recognizing the great arc of seasons, but then he said something that still haunts me to this day, something that bespeaks the belonging together of the diversity of human ways of knowing: "But Pythagoras says that something is still *the same.*"

This wasn't the time to remind him of the squares of sides on right-angled triangles, because that wasn't the way of knowing at hand. That was a way of knowing about the methods of operation of established science, to which those very methods of operation were no longer especially adequate. This is not logico-mathematical knowledge alone that this young boy is experiencing. It is the ancestral wisdom of such knowledge—this mathematician-philosopher, Pythagoras, has handed us some secret knowledge. Pythagoreans formed a secret cult in ancient Greece because they had found a mathematical key to something that always stays the same. They had found, one could say, one of the faces of God.

GLOSSARY

Analogical thinking—thinking by resemblance, according to kind and similarity, rather than law and identity. Things that fit together "by analogy" are parallel, similar, not identical.

Animism—The belief that anything that moves or is animate is alive.

Artificialism—The belief that anything that exists must have been created or caused or constructed by someone.

Some Cautionary Notes on Jean Piaget's Genetic Epistemology

Development: Belonging or Breakdown?

> The way we treat a thing can sometimes change its nature. (Hyde, 1983, xiii)

> There are no "pure facts" if by "facts" are meant phenomena presented nakedly to the mind by nature itself, independently respectively of the hypothesis by means of which the mind examines them and of the systematic framework of existing judgements into which the observer pigeon-holes every new observation. (Piaget, 1974a, p. 33)

> The old unilateral options of gericentrism (appealing to the authority of age, convention, tradition, nostalgia) and pedocentrism (child-centered pedagogy) only produce monstrous states of siege which are irresponsible to the matters at hand, that is, to the question of how life is mediated through relations between old and young. (Smith, 1988, p. 174; re-printed in Smith, 1999)

In educational theory and practice, we have a choice when it comes to how we might treat the generous legacy that Jean Piaget has handed us. We can start

with the individuality of the child and try to understand his or her developmental make-up: "where the child is at," as goes the educational adage. On that basis, we can then separate the disciplines that are entrusted to educators into corresponding developmentally sequenced parts and make these developmentally appropriate materials available in developmental sequence to the individual child. With the child and the child's developmental means at the centre of our considerations, we can divide and arrange the world (of reading, of writing, of mathematics and so on) around the child, in accordance with our understanding of this individualised centre. And, in the process of watching the child work and testing the results of our intervention, we can more accurately "target" what to do next.

This way of treating the legacy of developmentalism can result in teaching practices that have a very recognizable, and, I suggest, pedagogically unsound, character. With reading, for example, we end up having files full of developmentally colour-coded readers, each of which has been specifically designed to developmentally follow the others but no one of which contains a story actually worth reading. It has come to mean, in practice, that we present children with sequenced mathematics worksheets, each geared to the development and practice of an isolated skill (adding, subtracting, adding two-digit numbers and so on) when in fact, in the world of mathematics, no such isolation actually exists.

In both these cases, the world of language and the world of mathematics are subjected to what could be called a *developmental breakdown,* the very sort of breakdown required by established science as its central "method of operation":

> The object [reading, writing, mathematics] is disassembled, the rules of its functioning are ascertained, and then it is reconstructed according to those rules; so, also, knowledge is analysed, its rules are determined, and finally it is redeployed as method. The purpose of both [of these analytical breakdowns] is to prevent unanticipated future breakdowns by means of breaking down the object

even further and then synthesizing it [putting it back together in strictly in light of the demands of the method of operation of established science]. (Weinsheimer, 1987, p. 5)

This process of "breaking down even further" is precisely what has happened to Piaget's legacy of work. His legacy has, in many schools, turned into rigid, lockstep developmental sequences in our understanding of children and their ways of knowing. In parallel, it has turned into equally rigid developmental reconstructions of the living disciplines entrusted to schools. By presenting to the developmentally isolated individual child materials that are developmentally geared to his or her developmental level, we have, in effect, "prevent[ed] unanticipated future breakdowns" by having already broken down "reading" into its developmental parts and doled them out in a developmentally appropriate way—we have acted pre-emptively. The purple colour-coded reader is not too hard for this individual child, and not too soft. It's just right: just difficult and challenging enough to, in Piagetian terms, disturb the child's current assimilatory schemata and cause the accommodations required to lead to the next level of equilibration, the next stage of development.

Once the developmental sequences (of reading, of mathematics, of the child's development) are set, there will still be future breakdowns, but they will no longer be precisely unanticipated. If something unanticipated occurs when the child reads the purple "reading" book, that simply calls for analysing the situation in more developmental detail, for more accurate targeting of his or her developmental skills, for further divisions or subdivisions of skills and stages, for more severe and systematic isolation of tasks, materials or expectations, for different, more accurate testing procedures, and so on.

In cases like this, the outcome of the analytic process of "breaking things down" into their component parts (requisite of the way of knowing of established science) is to break apart the experiences that our children are offered in school, as wit-

nessed in those little colour-coded readers. This process actually treats reading as if it were the object of a scientific investigation. And, of course, it treats the children all around us in the very same way, as objects with developmental "properties" (constructed in line with, say, Piagetian theory). It presents children with a version of reading-sequenced, colour-coded developmental readers—the outcome of a logico-mathematical way of knowing that developmentalism suggests young children do not especially experience, have not learned, have no interest in, and are not developmentally capable of understanding.

As Piaget has taught us, this way of treating reading *changes its nature* by demanding that reading live up to the criteria of being an object of logico-mathematical breakdown. The world of reading, in all the ways we and our children have of knowing it and experiencing it and understanding it as part of the great human inheritance, is replaced with an objective developmental sequence of isolated skills and activities, all geared to the individual child and his or her developmental "needs."

It could even be said that this way of taking up Piaget's legacy of developmentalism can produce an unintended consequence: *breaking down* children into objectively determined clusters of "developmental needs," *breaking down* the community of the classroom into "developmental groupings," and *breaking down* the interrelatedness of the living disciplines—again, all with beneficent pedagogical intent.

Certainly this sort of developmental parsing (of children's ways of knowing, and of the curriculum areas entrusted to schools) can help a teacher identify and clarify aspects of writing, reading and mathematics, as well as aspects of children's coming to know such matters. But to then attempt to *teach* by immersing developmentally isolated children in the isolated, analytical results of this developmental parsing of the living disciplines is odd indeed.

But what, then, are we to do? Are we supposed to ignore the developmental needs of children and treat them like little adults? Doesn't this erase the sense of the uniqueness of children's ways of knowing? Of each individual child's special ways? Are we supposed to pile on tasks and demands irrespective of children and their needs and abilities? Isn't this teacher-centeredness or discipline-centeredness at its worst?

All of these are real danger, but we have another way to take up the grand legacy of Jean Piaget's insights. Let's try an analogy here. When I used to go out into the garden with my seven-year-old son, I didn't send him off to a "developmentally appropriate garden." I took him to the same garden where I was going to work, a garden full of a whole array of work to be done, things to be experienced, lessons to learn, tools to use, knowledge to apply and to cultivate and enrich. And so, too, worms came there, and ravens, and deer, and bears, each with their own ways, each with their own abilities and experiences, each with their own work to do. Now, once my son and I got to the garden and got to the work that place needed from us, of course we worked as each of us was able. We were not identical in ability, experience, strength, knowledge, wisdom, patience and so on. But *both of us* were working *in the same place,* doing some part of the real work that the garden requires, each cultivating the garden and ourselves in ways that are different and yet somehow belong together—akin, one might say (see chapter 4). That place where we met and worked together was rich and generous enough, full of enough possibilities of exploration and work, to embrace and hold together our differences in relations of kind (see Jardine, Clifford & Friesen, 2003a, 111–12). It allowed my son's ways of working, knowing and experiencing—and mine—to fully show themselves. And, of course, I learned something about that place and my own ways of knowing and experiencing it by living in the presence of my son's ways of knowing and experiencing it (and vice versa).

Each person's work in the classroom can be

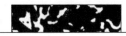

treated in an analogous fashion. This or that particular child's ways of knowing and engaging in the work of reading, for example, need not be treated as a subjective or interior possession. They can be treated as something that happens out in the whole *world* of reading—with others, in the presence of others and their work in this place. Each person's work, in all its individuality and uniqueness, is therefore taken up as adding to the richness of the place in which we find ourselves living together, in all our differences. We can fill the classroom and children's lives with generous, multileveled experiences of reading, writing and storytelling, and we can, in and through this diverse place, allow the differences of individual children to appear not in (developmental) isolation but in the midst and presence of all those participating in the work at hand.

In such a place, we can let go of "learning to read" as only an underdeveloped *child's* problem. We can recognize that reading itself is difficult and that the struggles children have with this way of knowing are just like the problems adults might have in reading, say, the "Kant" chapter of this book. This way of treating the Piagetian legacy allows us to experience children's struggles, not as developmentally isolated phenomena but as *belonging to* a long, ongoing, intergenerational history, an ancestry of human work (see Jardine, Clifford & Friesen, 2003, p. 119), work to which we as adults and teachers also belong in our own ways. .

I recall a first-grade class in which a student-teacher, himself a recent first-generation Vietnamese immigrant, was asked by his practicum teacher to read the book *Jeremiah Learns to Read* (Bogart, 1999). In this book, an old man is helped with his own tough work of learning to read by a class of young children undergoing the same struggle. The old man, in turn, teaches the children to "read" and recognize and imitate the sounds of geese and chickadees.

The student-teacher's first and understandable reaction was, of course, "What do you want me to teach them?"

The practicum teacher's response was telling: "I don't know yet. Don't try to teach them anything. Read them the book and talk with them about how difficult it is to learn to read. Talk to them about your own struggles. Don't 'teach' them. Just have a conversation with them; talk with them about the struggles and breakthroughs they've had, and about what you yourself know about the struggles and breakthroughs of learning to read."

This lesson helped the children in that class recognize that their own struggles with reading were part of something larger, something more complex and interesting. It helped them take up their own struggles with reading with a sense of relief from burden of isolation. Their troubles were not "kid troubles" but were just like Jeremiah's troubles, just like their new teacher's troubles. This classroom conversations and the work that followed, so to speak, "depathologized" their troubles and allowed them to be experienced as worldly troubles that can be shared and commiserated over. The long periods of brow-knitting practice became experienced and shareable as more than a mere aggregate of isolated subjective constructions or "developmental difficulties." Reading, in this context, becomes a world of trouble, a world of successes and failures, a world of work in which each of us has a part. As a result, that Vietnamese student-teacher was able to experience how he, too, brought something irreplaceable to our understanding and exploration of this place called "reading." And, too, the regular classroom teacher came to understand something about the world of reading and how her children inhabit it— how she, too, inhabits it—that she could not have otherwise understood.

The same way of treating Jean Piaget's legacy was at work in wonderful classroom discussions in a second-grade class where, in discussing stories about the Middle Ages, the children realized that King Arthur and the knights of the Round Table would probably not have known how to read. They learned that knowing how to read was something that most

adults did not know in these ancient times. They wanted the teachers to write down the names of monks, they wanted to read and reread descriptions of the *scriptorium,* to look over and handle plates of old illuminated manuscripts and details about why they were done that way, who did them, and why reading them might be a quite different experience than reading, say, this page in this book (see Illich, 1993). They wanted to talk about vellum, the calf-skins that were used for manuscripts, the compositions of inks, the making of scrolls and the meaning of their decoration (see Jardine, Graham, Clifford, & Friesen, 2002; Morrison, 2000). They wanted to produce an "illuminated" alphabet to replace the dull, store-bought one above the blackboard. They wanted to learn how to "read" the markings on shields and coats of arms for their hidden meanings. They were encouraged to "read" the paintings of Pieter Brueghel of village life at the end of the Middle Ages for clues as to what life might have been like. They were encouraged to read illustrations for clues as to what was written in the accompanying text, just as those in the Middle Ages might have learned to "read" the great allegories "written" in the stained-glass windows of the church. These children even designed their own stained-glass windows after great discussions about what they hoped people would be able to "read" in them when they were done. And these discussions were transcribed on large sheets of paper and hung up at the front of the class, made available for copying, questioning, checking spelling, or getting ideas to write about. The children were encouraged to use the sounds of letters to work out the words, both in writing and reading, just like we all do when first confronted with, for example, "Al-Qaeda" or "assimilatory schemata" or "transcendental logic." They learned about how unreliable English is when it comes to "sounding it out" and how this mongrel ancestry is itself inscribed into the history of the Middle Ages. They had intense discussions with recently immigrated Chinese children in the classroom about how, with Chinese characters, the issue of "sounding it out" makes no sense and what you do when the language you are learning to read and write seems to be composed of composites of pictures you recognize instead of clusters of sounds.

I even talked one day about how "medieval" is from the Latin *medium aevum,* "the middle era, the middle age." And, of course, they wanted to write that down and take it home and talk about the Latin they learned in second grade.

Also during the Middle Ages, the Roman numeral system was slowly being replaced with the Arabic numeral system that we still use. And so place-value showed up, as did that most dangerous idea, zero. And, too, in these difficult political days, one child asked a question whose consequences are yet to be fully worked out: "The numbers we use are *Arabic?*" If we had stuck to our developmental business, this gift—yet another place full of reading, writing, mathematics, issues of culture, diversity, difference, ancestry and place—would have never arrived.

In the midst of both these classrooms, it must be noted, a particular child still has his or her own particular troubles, and these troubles must be attended to with great care, but they are now visible in a context abundant with possible solutions. In a rich place—a rich "topic," as in "topography"— like the Middle Ages, there are many ways to enter into and take up the task of reading.

In this way of proceeding in the classroom, our actions are no longer meant to narrow attention, isolating children and the topic, and break things down. Our actions, rather, expand the depth, diversity and lived reality of the topics ("places") we take our children in the classroom. Jean Piaget's legacy is still significant here. It can help teachers to become sensitive to and understand the nuances children bring. It can help teachers understand that the knowledge children cultivate in this place is genuinely knowledge *of this place,* not some trivial "kids' work" done only because you don't yet know. Children and their ways of knowing, questioning and exploring are not developmental strangers living in some

developmentally portioned-off world. Rather, "there are children all around us"—here, for example, in the world of the Middle Ages, each working his way through this topic, this topography, in her own unique way.

Both of these ways of working in the classroom—breakdown or belonging—can lay claim to the legacy of Piaget. The way we treat a thing can sometimes change its nature.

On the Belonging of Established Science

This more "ecological/topographical" (see chapter 4; also see Jardine, Clifford & Friesen, 2003a; Jardine, 2000) way of treating the legacy of Piaget's work can be extended into a critique of that very legacy.

Piaget's descriptions of the "methods of operation" of established science demonstrate how, in order to give a reliable account of its results, science must remain within the confines of that way of knowing. We are all familiar with the language of "contamination" and "despoiling results" in established science. Hence, as cited in chapter 4, James Watson says, after his fireplace imaginings of floating DNA helixes, "Pretty. And hopefully scientific." Within the method of operation of science, the beauty of his image and the contingent circumstances in which he first imagined it are *irrelevant*. Also irrelevant is the long and complex history of the image of helixes and how this image was available to Watson as a way of understanding what he was seeing—a way of understanding inherited in our language and in our imagination from Latin and originally from the Greek *eilyein,* "to wrap or roll." Equally irrelevant are the drawings that Watson might have been arguing over, trying to picture the shape of DNA; the blackboards full of diagrams; heated conversations with colleagues; long hours reading relevant literature, searching out and testing various experimental designs; the bodily tiredness and frustration; the sip of single-malt Scotch; the trouble maintaining research funding and finding suit-

able outlets for the publication of results; all the politically and economically and personality/status charged quarrels over who was "first author," all the hope, the despair, the joys, the breakthroughs.

So here is a paradox. Such messy, contingent, circumstantial, worldly things—such imaginal, bodily, concrete, speculative, economic, cultural, political, motivated and philosophical ways of knowing and experiencing—are *not* irrelevant to the actual eventual accomplishment of the scientific discovery of the double-helix shape of DNA molecules. Established science, despite its "self sufficient" (Piaget, 1970b, p. 5) and "intrinsically intelligible" (p. 4) method of operation, does its work right here, in the world. But the "circumstances" *do not* and *cannot* appear as *part of* that accomplishment, because established science demands that its accomplishments *begin* only once its "method of operation" is enacted. In established science's account of its scientific accomplishments, these surrounding worldly events— these other ways of knowing and living in the world that surround its work and make its work possible—do not and cannot appear. Such an appearance would despoil the logico-mathematical method of operation that defines the study as scientific. After all, that book that I've cited by James Watson is autobiographical, not "scientific."

Piaget is quite clear on this point: "Science begins as soon as the problem can be isolated in such a way as to relate its solution to investigations that are universally accessible and verifiable, dissociating them from questions of evaluation and conviction" (Piaget, 1974b, p. 20).

And, further, established science necessarily follows "the essential rule of only asking questions in such terms that [logico-mathematically framed] verification and agreement is possible" (Piaget, 1965a, p. 12). However, the actual *doing* of established science as part of the human enterprise is itself not possible without all the complexities of ways of knowing in the midst of which it operates. The complex ways of knowing that Jean Piaget's work has identified,

therefore, do not simply form a developmental sequence that (ontogenetically or phylogenetically) *precedes* established science. This complex array of ways of knowing surrounds, houses and makes possible established science in ways that Piaget himself does not particularly address. At work here is what Hans Reichenbach, in *Experience and Prediction: An Analysis of the Foundations and the Structure of Knowledge* (1938), described as the difference between the "context of discovery" that surrounds established science and its self-defined, logico-mathematically delimited context of justification. "Pretty" is part of the context of discovery, but it does not help *justify* the double-helix character of DNA as a scientific finding.

Perhaps Piaget's work does not give us a good picture of the development of the actual operation of established science as a human enterprise but only a picture, so to speak, of its ways of justifying its results, a justification that has deliberately purged itself of the very complexity of ways of knowing that it in fact deeply relies upon. Or has it?

> Rosalind Franklin, a micro-chemist, was the first person to discover the structure of the DNA molecule but as a female Jew in an all-male scientific organization, her colleagues, Maurice Wilkins, James Watson and Francis Crick, refused to give her credit. Wilkins gave Franklin's data to Watson and Crick without her permission and would not allow her to attend their meetings to discuss her results. Wilkins would not accept females in the doctoral program he supervised as late as the 1970s. Franklin was unable to share in the 1962 Nobel Prize with them because she died of cancer in 1958, and only living people can receive a Nobel Prize. Not only did she discover the helical structure of DNA, she showed Watson the mistakes in his original double-helix model which led to his award-winning conclusions. (Vare & Ptacek, 1988, 214–15)

So much for the lovely story about fireplaces and helix imaginings. Maybe this is feminism exaggeration and distortion. Or maybe it's the truth finally out. Certainly it is no wonder that Piaget's work focuses only on what occurs within the confines of the method of operation of established science. What occurs beyond those confines is often difficult indeed, with no clear and controllable methodology to help us sort out once and for all what its "single truth alone" might be. This just may be precisely the sort of life-world "surrounding" established science— how it is actually accomplished, only one part of which is its internal, logico-mathematical method of justification—that we want children to know about in our school curriculum. After all, coming up with a good hypothesis takes imagination, even though scientifically testing it does not. Cultivating children's ability to imagine is thus essential to their coming to master science, even though it is not essential to the ways of justifying scientific findings.

"The Sciences Are Self-Sufficient"

> The sciences are self-sufficient and alone guaran-tee their own reflection. (Piaget, 1965a, p. 225)

> [Established science involves] an ideal, perhaps a hope, of intrinsic intelligibility supported by the postulate that the structures are self-sufficient and that to grasp them, we do not have to make refer-ence to all sorts of extraneous elements. (Piaget, 1970b, pp. 4–5)

We can rest assured that Piaget knew full well that established science has grown up out of the history of the human species, that it must also grow up out of the life of the developing child, and that it grows, too, up out of the life of the scientist who lives in the world in ways that go beyond the confines of his or her eventual scientific work.

The question now is, what does it grow up *into?*

Here Piaget's legacy takes a difficult turn and inter-weaves with darker images and more troubled dreams. As we discussed above, Piaget believes that by grow-ing into established science, humanity grows into self-sufficiency, independence, objectivity, disinterestedness, renunciation, "maturity." As we dis-covered in chapter 3, in Piaget's work, the concepts, categories and methods of established science are not

simply an adaptation that belongs among and is surrounded and sustained by others. Science is, he contends, "an *extension* and *perfection* of all adaptive processes" (Piaget, 1973, p. 7). Human intelligence as manifest in the concepts, categories and methods of established science is the crowning moment of "life itself." More strongly put, it is that adaptation, that way of constructing an understanding of the world, toward which life itself strives.

To help tease out these ideas, let's begin with a passage from a very early work that Piaget wrote as a nineteen-year-old during the ravages of the First World War. In this prose-poem, titled "The Mission of the Idea," Piaget lays out great themes that will define his life's work and that therefore underwrite the legacy inherited by educational theory and practice:

> Life is good, but the individual pursuing his self-interest renders it bad. Every individual instinctively, unconsciously serves its species, serves life. But self-interest may lead the individual to keep for himself some of the vital energy which he might bring to others. One day intelligence appeared, illuminated life, opening new domains to mankind. But here again self-interest appeared, now armed with reason. But man, having tasted of the fruits of the tree of life, remains caught in this conflict between self-interest and renunciation (Piaget, 1977, pp. 29–30).

This early hymn to God, to life, to humanity at its best, finds amazing echoes in Piaget's later descriptions of the nature of the "renunciation" of "self-interest" that is central to established science. This renunciation occurs through the transformation of the self, over the course of development, from a self-centred subject to an anonymous, replaceable, "disinterested" subject who operates solely in terms of "processes common to all subjects" (Piaget, 1965a, p. 108). Thus:

> A distinction must be at once drawn between the individual subject, centred on his sense organs or on his own actions—and hence on the ego or egocentric subject as a source of possible deforma-

tion or illusion of the "subjective" type in the basic meaning of the term—and the decentred subject who coordinates his actions as between them and those of others; who measures, calculates, and deduces in a way that can be generally verified; and whose epistemic activities are therefore common to all subjects, even if they are replaced by electronic or cybernetic machines with a built-in logical and mathematical capacity similar to that of the human brain. (Piaget, 1973, pp. 7–8)

This "decentred subject" is still a human subject, but it is now a subject who operates not according to self-interest but according to and only in terms of the method of operation of established science—only in terms of the essential nature of the inevitable "organizing activity inherent in life itself" (Piaget, 1952, p. 19), deployed deliberately as its *method*. This method "serves life" (Piaget, 1977, p. 30) by cleaving solely and strictly to its essential, invariant nature (the universal and necessary functional *a priori*). Through such "decentration," in which we move away from self-interest, we "no longer intervene as an individual or distorting subject, but as an epistemic subject, the condition and instrument of objectivity" (Piaget, 1967, p. 338). "As long as one does not seek verification by a group of facts established experimentally or by deduction conforming to an exact algorithm (as in logic)," Piaget argues, "the criterion of truth can only remain subjective" (1965a, p. 12).

To push this one step further, through the development of such "decentration," we become more and more alike, and, eventually, as the anonymous wielders of logico-mathematical knowledge, we become *identical*. The development of the child can thus be understood as the *overcoming of difference,* the very differences that Piaget's genetic epistemology has so carefully detailed and explored.

Piaget's work is clearly still full of old Enlightenment ideals regarding established science. Science is the crowning jewel of humanity, the sign of humanity's maturity, its independence, reliability, reasonableness, logicalness, constancy, self-sufficiency, trustworthiness and so on. It may not be

abstractly understandable as an "independent absolute" (Piaget, 1952, p. 19) but stands among other ways as the most mature, the least self-interested, the most independent and self sufficient, perfectly "self-regulating" (Piaget, 1971b, p. 26), since the terms of its self-regulation are the organizing activity inherent in life itself, and the "self" accomplishing such regulation is the "epistemic subject" who works only in accord with this method of operation.

It is at this juncture that Immanuel Kant, Piaget's forebearer, is helpful once again in understanding what is at play in his descendant's work. In Kant's description of the central call of the Enlightenment, images of maturity and immaturity, of adulthood and childhood appear:

> *Enlightenment is man's emergence from his self-imposed immaturity. Immaturity* is the inability to use one's understanding without guidance from another. This immaturity is *self-imposed* when its cause lies not in a lack of understanding, but in a lack of resolve and courage to use it without guidance from another. *Sapere Aude!:* "Have courage to use your own understanding!"—that is the motto of the Enlightenment. (1964, p. 41, emphasis original)

We find similar images of adult and child, of maturity and immaturity (even of teacher and pupil) buried in a previously cited passage from Kant's *Critique of Pure Reason,* part of which is worth re-citing here:

> A light broke upon the students of nature. They learned that reason has insight only into that which it produces after a plan of its own, and that it must not allow itself to be kept, as it were, in nature's leading-strings, but must itself show the way with principles of judgement based on fixed laws, constraining nature to give answer to questions of reason's own determining. Reason . . . must approach nature in order to be taught by it. It must not, however, do so in the character of a pupil who listens to everything the teacher chooses to say, but of an appointed judge who compels the witnesses to answer questions which he had himself formulated. (Kant, 1964, p. 20)

Here we get images of the heretofore dependent

pupil turning away from his teachers and their guidance (one meaning of "leading strings" is "pupilage" or "being led or taught by another"). Under the Enlightenment ideal, *any* guidance other than that demanded by reason itself (in Piaget's work, demanded by the method of operation of established science) is ruled out as indicative of childishness or immaturity. Another image buried here is one of the boy cutting the leading-strings (or "apron strings") that bind him to nature (that is, to his mother—another age-old allegorical thread to be explored). Once achieved, reason (in Kant's work) and established science (in Piaget's work) have no lingering dependency on anything that has given rise to them, given "birth" to them, one might say.

The Enlightenment image of reason, then, is pictured as the way in which humanity has overcome its immaturity or primitiveness; in Piaget's work, "the child is the real primitive among us, the missing link between prehistorical men and contemporary adults" (Voneche & Bovet, 1982, p. 88; also see Malvern, 1994; Nandy, 1983). The child is the embodied primitive, suggesting wildness and animality ("leading-strings" also refers to a cord used to lead and train animals). Alice Miller (1989) has traced in detail how what she called the "black pedagogies" of the eighteenth and nineteenth centuries understood children to be wild and wilful beings who must be made to "mind," who must be "taught a lesson." If we begin with the belief that we are in command of the categories of maturity and civility that define the crowning jewel of humanity, we can believe as well that we are able—in fact *morally obligated*—to use any means necessary to bring our children in line with our preordained destiny. And all of this will be done, of course, with beneficent intent: *For Your Own Good* (Miller, 1989).

Once the leading-strings are cut, we can finally "stand on our own two feet" ("leading-strings" were used to teach children to stand and walk; this image is also used as a metaphor for "dependency"). Again from Jean Piaget's "The Mission of the Idea" (1977,

pp. 30–31): "The child on the point of becoming a man is irresolute and weak, his soul is in turmoil, painful no matter how beautiful its mysterious source. From this crisis comes a mature fruit, thus is born humanity." We have now stepped fully into dangerous territories.

When Piaget (1971a, pp. 12–14) speculated that ontogeny (the stages of growth of the individual) might recapitulate phylogeny (the stages of growth of the species), he was not deliberately contending that our ancestors were like children, or that those from cultures and ways other than Enlightenment Europe might be full of the naiveté, immaturity and petulance of childhood. He is not deliberately suggesting that those who do not heed the Enlightenment call

> [B]elong to a different mentality: savage, primitive, underdeveloped, backwards, alienated, composed of opinions, customs, authority, prejudice, ignorance, ideology. Narratives are fables, myths, legends, fit only for women and children. At best, attempts are made to throw some rays of light into this obscurantism, to civilize, educate, develop. (Usher and Edwards, 1994, p. 158)

And yet, of course, this is precisely the legacy we are currently living out, a legacy of which Jean Piaget's work is, however unwittingly and however unintended, a part. His work emerged in the wake of deeply imperial, deeply colonial, deeply self-confident and assured images of how the world works and how the peoples of the world are to be understood in light of the crowning achievement of European Enlightenment and European (and now North American) images of civility, democracy, reasonableness and liberty.

"The Savage Childhood of the Human Race"

This surely isn't the place to even attempt to untangle all of the threads of these issues. For now, I'll offer only a sketch, a beginning caution.

We have all witnessed how the language of "development" has come to be used in our under-

standing of the diversity of cultures and peoples in the world. We know full well this history. For example, we know how, under the British Empire, the diversity of the Commonwealth was spread before the Crown as a wonderful, rich array of comparatively uncivilized, underdeveloped, less reasonable, less cultured, less "mature" places. We know from the work of Ashish Nandy (1983; 1987) how those subjected to colonial rule were systematically and deliberately characterized as "children." We are surrounded by an increasing number of critiques of these images of development:

> [W]hen underdeveloped countries are called "developing" countries, it's a way of saying they are like children—growing, developing. And it's a lie. They are underdeveloped because more powerful countries are growing at their expense. Third World underdevelopment is a consequence of First World development, and not a stage toward it. (Galeano, 2000)

Eduardo Galeano (1997, p. 30) thus gives us pause over the image of "belonging" that we have too easily and too happily toyed with in Jean Piaget's legacy: "The one [developed] and the other [underdeveloped] make up the same system."

There is no good reason to map out the historical unfolding of things (phylogeny) unless it proves to be the case that "we" are the fulfilment, the flowering, the most developed, the most civilized. Unfolding the course of historical movement is always done, first of all, under the belief that there is an undeniable maturity and civility *already possessed* by those pursuing such unfoldings. Developmentalism is not possible in a culture that does not view itself thus. You don't map out a sequence in order to find that you are the "Third" World but only to show what you already believe, that you are "number one."

Developmentalism does not seek out the past ("previous stages," both ontogenetic and phylogenetic) in order to help us live our lives on the basis of generously knowing and learning from living

among ancestors, living among children, living among a diversity of cultures and beliefs. It seeks out development in order to help substantiate the belief that "we" have *fulfilled* our ancestry. "We" are its proper *end*. We can thus act pre-emptively vis-à-vis "the immature" because we already know what their future holds (just as we can imagine those little colour-coded readers in first grade as a pre-emptive understanding of what children's future development holds in store).

Buried here is another thread with echoes of Piaget's: "modernity is a single condition, everywhere the same and always benign. As societies become more modern, so they become more alike. At the same time, they become better" (Gray, 2003, p. 1). What societies become more like is defined, of course, by "the winners of the world" (Nandy, 1983, p. 47) because, to use Piaget's terminology, having become a winner of the world means precisely that the winner's ways of knowing and acting are more "adaptive" than the losers whose destiny it is to be eventually erased. The winners of the world are more mature, more civilized, less childish and self-centred.

Developmentalism thus adds a profound twist to the old colonialism. Under colonialism, we were able to believe that we stood in the midst of the world as the best—the freest, the most reasonable, the most civilized. Under developmentalism, we get a new twist on the modernist spirit of universality and necessity (recall, Kant's criteria for the *a priori*): we are not just "the best" among others in the world, the most civilized, the most literate, the most moral, the most "free " (all old colonial cants). If we add "development" to the modern spirit, we are that *toward which* the world is developing, naturally and of natural necessity. With the addition of "development" to the modernist idea of universality, we become "mature," and the "developing world" becomes not only immature but inevitably heading our way. "Underdeveloped nations" (as becomes the euphemism) become like not-yet-fully developed children whose future we already understand and embody, children who are in need of nurturing,

love, encouragement—and strict discipline.

Just in case this interpretation seems to be getting a bit out of hand, consider the following excerpt from an interview with David Frum, a Canadian and the author of George W. Bush's "axis of evil" speech. In speaking with Evan Solomon, one of the hosts of the Canadian Broadcasting Company's (CBC) television program *Sunday Morning,* Frum was attempting to lay out his vision of the place of past and future American pre-emptive actions in the Middle East. Images of childhood, adolescence and adulthood—images of development—appear:

EVAN SOLOMON: Is this a prescription for American imperialism? Is this the new empire? I know that you think it is a beneficent empire. . . .

DAVID FRUM: No, no, absolutely not. This is the adolescence of the human race. This is the moment when human beings are making the transition from a world governed by violence to a world governed by law. Just as the North Atlantic is governed by law, we hope that some day the whole world will look like that. But the instrument whereby humanity is going to make that transition from the savage childhood of the human race to law-abiding adulthood is through the instrument of American power. It is America who is going to . . . maybe someday it will be somebody else's . . . maybe someday it will be India's job, a while ago it was Britain's, but today it is America's power that is going to spread the realm of law and civilization and democracy. (Frum & Solomon, 2004)

Perhaps there are ways that the troubled legacy of Jean Piaget's work can help us hear what is at work in such statements.

A Final Pedagogical Mediation on Jean Piaget's Legacy

In my role in teacher-education, I have been talking with student-teachers about a disturbing and yet inevitable aspect of teaching: that the stu-

dents you teach *think about you* in ways that you might not think about yourself, that they experience and know the world in ways that go beyond our own. A first response might be, of course, bewilderment, paranoia, withdrawal, humiliation, anger, even violence. However, students are often able to read our hopes, intentions and experiences back to us in ways that have the potential to release us from the potentially deadly and deadening enclosures of our own self-narration.

This is a huge revelation for a new teacher: that we might listen to others, not only in order to understand *them* and what *they* believe better but in order to understand *ourselves* better, to understand what *we* believe in ways that we could have never understood alone. It may be that it is precisely the release from the enclosures of our own self-narration that makes teaching and learning possible. Only in such release can we understand ourselves as living with others in the great, ongoing, sometimes terrifying, sometimes joyful conversation that constitutes being human. Our only hope just might be the realization that "genuine life together is made possible only in the context of an ongoing conversation which is never over yet which also must be sustained for life together to go on at all" (Smith, 1988, p. 176.

This, perhaps, is Jean Piaget's greatest and most troublesome gift to those of us in education: that we are not just knowing but known. We are not just experiencing others but experienced by them. Our ability to take up this challenge with love and affection—"kind-ness," one might call it, to use our terms from chapter 4—despite all the sometimes overwhelming difficulties that challenge entails, might be the greatest test of our "maturity."

References

Aristotle, *Metaphysics*. Book IV. http://vms.cc.wmich.edu/~mcgrew/aristotle.htm (accessed January 10, 2004.

Ausubel, D. P., Sullivan, E. V., & Ives, S. W. (1980). *Theory and problems of child development.* New York: Grune & Stratton.

Bogart, J.E. (1999). *Jeremiah learns to read.* New York: Orchard Books.

Clifford, P., & Friesen, S. (2003). A curious plan: Managing on the twelfth. In Jardine et al., *Back to the basics* (pp. 15–36).

Dressman, M. (1993). Lionizing lone wolves: The cultural romantics of literacy workshops. *Curriculum Inquiry, 23(3)*, 239–63.

Eliade, M. (1968). *Myth and reality.* New York: Harper & Row.

Elkind, D. (1967). Introduction to J. Piaget, *Six psychological studies* (v–xviii). New York: Vintage Books.

Frum, D. & Solomon, E. (2004, January 18). Interview. *Sunday morning* [Television broadcast]. Toronto ON: Canadian Broadcasting Company.

Galeano, E. (1997). *Open veins of Latin America: Five centuries of the pillage of a continent.* New York: Monthly Review Press.

———. (2000, November 30). An interview. *Atlantic Unbound.* http://www.theatlantic.com/unbound/interviews/ba200 0–11–30.htm (accessed January 1, 2004).

Gardner, H. (2000). *Intelligence reframed: multiple intelligences for the 21st century.* Toronto: HarperCollins Canada / Basic Books.

Grant, G. (1998). *English-speaking justice.* Toronto: House of Anansi Press.

Gray, J. (2003). *Al Qaeda and what it means to be modern.* New York: The New Press.

Gruber, H. & Voneche, J. J., Eds. (1977). *The essential Piaget.* New York: Basic Books.

Haeckel, E. (1900). *Riddle of the universe at the close of the nineteenth century.* New York: Harper Brothers.

Heidegger, M. (1985). *The history of the concept of time.* Bloomington: Indiana University Press.

Hillman, J. (1983). *Healing fiction.* Barrytown, NY: Station Hill Press.

Hyde, L. (1983). *The gift: Imagination and the erotic life of property.* New York: Vintage Books.

Illich, I. (1993). *In the vineyard of the text: A commentary on Hugh's "Didascalicon."* Chicago: University of Chicago Press.

Indiana University. http://www.indiana.edu/~intell/piaget.html. (accessed July 14, 2005).

Inhelder, B. (1969). Some aspects of Piaget's genetic approach to cognition. In H. Furth (Ed.), *Piaget and knowledge: Theoretical foundations* (pp. 9–23). Englewood Cliffs, NJ: Prentice-Hall.

Jardine, D. W. (1994). The ecologies of mathematics and the rhythms of the earth. In P. Ernest (Ed.), *Studies in Mathematics Education: Vol. 3. Mathematics, philosophy and education: An international perspective* (pp. 109–23). London: Falmer Press.

———. (1998). On the humility of mathematical language. In *"To dwell with a boundless heart": On curriculum theory, hermeneutics and the ecological imagination* (pp. 53–68). New York: Peter Lang.

———. (2000). *"Under the tough old stars": Ecopedagogical essays.* Vol. 4 of the Foundation for Educational Renewal series, catalogue number 4177. Brandon, VT: Psychology Press/Holistic Education Press.

———. (2002). Welcoming the old man home: A meditation on Jean Piaget, interpretation and the "nostalgia for the original." *Taboo: A Journal of Culture and Education, 6(1),* 5–21.

———. (2003). "Because it shows us the way at night": On animism, interpretation and the re-animation of Piagetian theory. In Jardine et al., *Back to the basics* (pp. 143–56).

———. (in press). "It followed him to school one day": Eight pedagogical preambles on Dolly the sheep. *Interchange: A Quarterly Review of Education.*

Jardine, D. & Morgan, G.A.V. (1987). Analogical thinking in young children and the use of logico-mathematical knowledge as a paradigm in Jean Piaget's genetic epistemology. *The Quarterly Newsletter of the Laboratory of Comparative Human Cognition, 9(4),* 95–101.

Jardine, D., Clifford, P., & Friesen, S., Eds. (2003a). *Back to the basics of teaching and learning: "Thinking the world together."* Mahwah, NJ: Lawrence Erlbaum and Associates.

Jardine, D., Friesen, S. & Clifford, P. (2003b). "Behind each jewel are three thousand sweating horses ": Meditations on the ontology of mathematics and mathematics education. In E. Hasebe-Ludt & W. Hurren (Eds.), *Curriculum intertext: Place/language/pedagogy* (pp. 39–50). New York: Peter Lang.

Jardine, D., Graham, T., Clifford, P. & Friesen, S. (2002). In his own hand: Interpretation and the effacing of the scribe. *Language and Literacy: A Canadian On-Line E-Journal.* http://educ.queensu.ca/~landl/web/archive/v01141/papers/jardine (accessed July 22, 2005).

Kant, I. (1964). *Critique of pure reason.* London: Macmillan.

———. (1983). *Perpetual peace and other essays.* Indianapolis, IN: Hackett.

Kohlberg, L. (1989). *The stages of ethical development: From childhood through old age.* Toronto: HarperCollins Canada.

Le Guin, U. (1987). *Buffalo gals and other animal presences.* Santa Barbara, CA: Capra Press.

Malvern, S. (1994). Recapping on recapitulation: How to primitivise the child. *The Third Text, 27* (summer), 21–30.

McClosky, R. (1976). *Blueberries for Sal.* London: Puffin Books.

Miller, A. (1989). *For your own good: Hidden cruelty in child-rearing and the roots of violence.* Toronto: Collins.

Morrison, B. (2000). *The justification of Johann Gutenberg.* Toronto: Random House of Canada.

Nandy, A. (1983). *The intimate enemy: Loss and recovery of self under colonialism.* Delhi: Oxford University Press.

———. (1987). *Traditions, tyranny and utopia.* Delhi: Oxford University Press.

Norris-Clarke, W. (1976). Analogy and the meaningfulness of language about God. *The Thomist, 40,* 61–95.

Piaget, J. (1952). *The Origins of intelligence in children.* New York: International Universities Press.

———. (1965a). *Insights and illusions of philosophy.* New York: Meridian Books.

———. (1965b). *Moral reasoning in the child.* New York: The Free Press.

———. (1967). *Six psychological studies.* New York: Vintage Books.

———. (1970a). Piaget's theory. In P. Mussen (Ed.), *Carmichael's manual of child psychology. Vol. 1* (pp. 703–32). Toronto: Wiley and Sons.

———. (1970b). *Structuralism.* New York: Harper and Row.

———. (1971a). *Genetic epistemology.* New York: W.W. Norton.

———. (1971b). *Biology and knowledge.* Chicago: University of Chicago Press.

———. (1971c). *The construction of reality in the child.* New York: Ballantine Books.

———. (1972a). *Judgement and reasoning in the child.* Totowa NJ: Littlefield and Adams.

———. (1972b). *The child's conception of physical causality.* Totowa, NJ: Littlefield and Adams.

———. (1973). *The psychology of intelligence.* Totowa, NJ: Littlefield, Adams and Co.

———. (1974a). *The child's conception of the world.* London: Paladin Books.

———. (1974b). *The place of the sciences of man in the system of science.* New York: Harper and Row.

———. (1974c). *The language and thought of the child.* New York: Meridian Books.

———. (1977). The mission of the idea. In Gruber & Voneche, *The essential Piaget* (26–37).

Piaget, J. & Evans, R. (1973). *Jean Piaget: The man and his ideas.* New York: E. P. Dutton and Co.

Piaget, J. & Inhelder, B. (1969). Gaps in empiricism. In Inhelder & Chipman, *Piaget and his school: A reader in developmental psychology.*

Popper, K. (2002). *The logic of scientific discovery.* New York: Routledge.

Reichenbach, H. (1938). *Experience and prediction: An analysis of the foundations and the structure of knowledge.* Chicago: University of Chicago Press.

Seife, C. (2000). *Zero: The biography of a dangerous idea.* New York: Penguin Books.

Shepard, P. (1996). *The others: How animals made us human.* Washington, DC: Island Press.

Smith, D. G. (1988). Children and the gods of war. *Journal of Educational Thought, 22A(2),* 173–77.

———. (1999). *Pedagon: Interdisciplinary essays in the human sciences, pedagogy and culture.* New York: Peter Lang.

Spock, B., & Parker, S. (1957). *Dr. Spock's Baby and Child Care.* New York: Cardinal Giant Edition.

Sudnow, D. (1979). *Ways of the hand.* New York: Bantam Books.

Usher, R. & Edwards, R. (1994). *Postmodernism and education.* London: Routledge.

Vare, E., & Ptacek, G. (1988). *Mothers of invention. From the bra to the bomb: Forgotten women and their unforgettable ideas.* New York: William Morrow and Co.

Voneche, J., & Bovet, M. (1982). Training research and cognitive development: What do Piagetians want to accomplish? In S. Modgil & C. Modgil (Eds.), *Jean Piaget: Consensus and controversy* (pp. 83–94). London: Holt, Rinehart and Winston.

Watson, J. (n. d.) *The double helix: A personal account of the discovery of the structure of DNA.* www.phy.bme.hu/~hild/helix/helix.pdf (accessed January 13, 2004).

Weinsheimer, J. (1987). *Gadamer's hermeneutics.* New Haven, CT: Yale University Press.

Wittgenstein, L. (1968). *Philosophical investigations.* Cambridge: Blackwell.

Additional Reference Material

There are literally thousands of books, articles and websites that deal with aspects of Jean Piaget's work. There are also thousands of available teacher resources organized (some-

times explicitly, sometimes not) around issues of children's "development." These texts and resources are by no means restricted to cognitive development (Jean Piaget's main interest). This list of additional reference material is thus necessarily brief.

General Information and Critiques

John Flavell provides synoptic overview of Jean Piaget's work. Clear, concise and descriptive up until the mid-1960s. Good descriptions of the stages of development and descriptions of Jean Piaget's own development, but this text provides no reference at all to educational matters.

Flavell, J. (1963). *Developmental psychology of Jean Piaget.* Princeton, NJ: Van Nostrand.

Another synoptic text which provides a case for the application of Jean Piaget's work to education and schools.

Furth, H. G., and H. Wachs. (1974). *Thinking goes to school.* New York: Oxford University Press.

Applications to Education

Anything by Eleanor Duckworth is worthwhile reading. Her work is rooted in Piagetian theory but critical of it in ways that provide wonderful examples and resources for educators.

Duckworth, E. R. (1979). "Either we're too early and they can't learn it or we're too late and they know it already": The dilemma of "applying Piaget." *Harvard Educational Review, 49,* 3.

———. (1987). *"The having of wonderful ideas" and other essays on teaching and learning.* New York: Teachers College Press.

Also worthwhile is the work of Constance Kamii and her coauthors. She details how Piagetian theory can help teachers understand children's developing understanding of mathematics and as well as gives specific activities and experiences that teachers can use both to "diagnose" children's work and to provide meaningful experiences for them.

Kamii, C., & De Clark, G. (1985). *Young children reinvent arithmetic: Implications of Piaget's theory.* New York: Teachers College Press.

Kamii, C., & Livingston, S. J. (1994). *Young children continue to reinvent arithmetic. Third grade: Implications of Piaget's theory.* New York: Teachers College Press.

Kamii, C., & Young, L. L. J. (1989). *Children continue to reinvent arithmetic. Second grade: Implications of Piaget's theory.* New York: Teachers College Press.

Another author who has provided sequenced, structured activities for classroom mathematics activities is Richard Skemp. Although Skemp is not strictly a Piagetian, he does focus on how real mathematics can be done in elementary-school classrooms instead of the often developmentally isolated and trivialized work that some practices support.

Skemp, R. (1989). *Structured activities for primary mathematics: How to enjoy real mathematics.* London: Routledge.

David Elkind is one of Jean Piaget's most articulate interpreters, and his work has become extremely influential. Although it is not tethered specifically to Jean Piaget's work, the following text in particular is highly recommended. It provides a compelling case for our tendency to not understand the slow, deliberate and unhurried character of children's development, and it details the very real dangers involved in our culture's rush to educate children irrespective of their ways in the world.

Elkind, D. (1981). *The hurried child: Growing up too fast too soon.* Reading, MA: Addison-Wesley.

Other wonderful books by Elkind follow.

Elkind, D. (1974). *Children and adolescents: Interpretive essays on Jean Piaget.* New York: Oxford University Press.

———. (1976). *Child development and education: A Piagetian perspective.* New York: Oxford University Press.

———. (1984). *All grown up and no place to go: Teenagers in crisis.* Reading, MA: Addison-Wesley.

———. (1987). *Mis-education: Preschoolers at risk.* New York: Knopf.

Piagetian theory has been applied to children's artwork and its development.

Kellogg, R. (1969). *Analyzing children's art.* Palo Alto, CA: National Press Books.

As mentioned in the book, Jean Piaget was briefly interested in moral development and moral reasoning, and this was taken up by Lawrence Kohlberg. This part of Jean Piaget's legacy was carefully critiqued by Carol Gilligan, who demonstrated how the adult model that was used to detail this development was specifically male in character.

Gilligan, C. (1982). *In a different voice: Psychological theory and women's development.* Cambridge, MA: Harvard University Press.

The Ancestries of Jean Piaget's Theory

As mentioned in the text, most resources on Jean Piaget are either applications of his ideas to education or critiques, refinements or expansions of his objective scientific work. These two resources deal specifically with the ancestral threads that underwrite Jean Piaget's work.

Goot, M. (1989). *Piaget as a visionary thinker.* Bristol, England: Wyndam Hall Press.

Vidal, F. (1994). *Piaget before Piaget.* Cambridge, MA. Harvard University Press.

Additional Articles by the Author on Jean Piaget and Development

Jardine, D. (1984). The Piagetian picture of the world. *Phenomenology + Pedagogy, 2(3),* 229–34.

———. (1987). Reflection and self-understanding in Piagetian theory: A phenomenological critique. *Journal of Educational Thought, 21(1),* 10–19.

———. (1988). "There are children all around us." *Journal of Educational Thought, 22(2A),* 178–86.

———. (1988). Piaget's clay and Descartes' wax. *Educational Theory, 38(3),* 287–98. Reprinted in *"Under the tough old stars": Ecopedagogical essays.* Brandon, VT: Psychology Press / Holistic Education Press (2000).

———. (1992). Immanuel Kant, Jean Piaget and the rage for order: Hints of the colonial spirit in pedagogy. *Educational Philosophy and Theory, 23(1),* 28–43. Reprinted in *"To dwell with a boundless heart": On curriculum theory, hermeneutics and the ecological imagination.* New York: Peter Lang Publishing (1998).

Jardine, D., & Morgan, G. (1987). Analogy as a model for the development of representational abilities in children. *Educational Theory, 37(3),* 209–18.

Friesen, S., Clifford, P., & Jardine, D. (1998). Meditations on community, memory and the intergenerational character of mathematical truth. *Journal of Curriculum Theorizing, 14(3),* 6–11. Reprinted in Jardine et al. (Eds.), *Back to the basics.*

Web Resources

For "official" Jean Piaget websites with dozens of links to articles and books as well as links to other relevant websites:

http://www.unige.ch/piaget/Presentations/presentg.html
(*the Jean Piaget Archives at the University of Geneva, which houses the Centre for the Study of Genetic Epistemology*)

http://www.piaget.org/ (*the Jean Piaget Society: Society for the Study of Knowledge and Development*)

For brief biographies of Jean Piaget:

http://www.crystalinks.com/piaget.html

http://www.fmarion.edu/psych/bio/piaget.htm

http://psychology.about.com/library/bl/blbio_piaget.htm

For descriptions of Jean Piaget's stages of cognitive development:

http://en.wikipedia.org/wiki/Jean_Piaget

http://www.child-reading-tips.com/ piaget's-stages-of-child-development.htm

http://www.indiana.edu/~intell/piaget.shtml

http://honolulu.hawaii.edu/intranet/committees/FacDevCom/guidebk/teachtip/piaget.htm

Peter Lang PRIMERS

in Education

Peter Lang Primers are designed to provide a brief and concise introduction or supplement to specific topics in education. Although sophisticated in content, these primers are written in an accessible style, making them perfect for undergraduate and graduate classroom use. Each volume includes a glossary of key terms and a References and Resources section.

Other published and forthcoming volumes cover such topics as:

- Standards
- Popular Culture
- Critical Pedagogy
- Literacy
- Higher Education
- John Dewey
- Feminist Theory and Education
- Studying Urban Youth Culture

- Multiculturalism through Postformalism
- Creative Problem Solving
- Teaching the Holocaust
- Piaget and Education
- Deleuze and Education
- Foucault and Education

Look for more Peter Lang Primers to be published soon. To order other volumes, please contact our Customer Service Department:

    800-770-LANG (within the US)
    212-647-7706 (outside the US)
    212-647-7707 (fax)

To find out more about this and other Peter Lang book series, or to browse a full list of education titles, please visit our website:

    www.peterlangusa.com